M000083655

When in Doubt - Always Choose Yourself!

A Simple Path to Make Sure You Eliminate Negative Thinking and Don't Let Others Put You Down Anymore!

Max J. Harrison

When in Doubt – Always Choose Yourself!

rendering of legal, financial, medical or professional advice. The content within this book has been derived from various sources. Please consult a licensed professional before attempting any techniques outlined in this book.

By reading this document, the reader agrees that under no circumstances is the author responsible for any losses, direct or indirect, which are incurred as a result of the use of the information contained within this document, including, but not limited to, — errors, omissions, or inaccuracies.

When in Doubt – Always Choose Yourself!

TABLE OF CONTENTS

When in Doubt – Always Choose Yourself!

Introduction

"Seeing the mud around a lotus is pessimism,
seeing a lotus in the mud is optimism."

Amit Kalantri

I assume that you have bought this book because you're interested in positive thinking, and soon I'm going to tell you exactly what this book is about, who I am, and precisely the type of people who will benefit from it.

But before I do any of that I need to state something that is important to understanding the subject of this book, and critical to allowing yourself to change your negative thought patterns.

It's this: Your "self" does not really exist. It is a construct, a by-product of your upbringing. Consequently, your thoughts are also constructs. And for those who suffer from negative thoughts, they are nothing but damaging vestiges from your past.

Let me explain. The first time I came across this notion of the "self" being a construct I railed against it. I dismissed it as ridiculous. What does

it mean, my "self" doesn't exist? Does that mean I don't exist, that I am a construct? Here I am, parked at my desk, my bottom squirming because the seat is too uncomfortable, sipping a lukewarm cup of coffee, and eyeing up a juicy-looking apple I fully intend to devour in about 10 minutes. This is my "self". To say it doesn't exist, or is a construct, is flat-out ridiculous.

Of course, our bodies exist; they occupy space, and the blood, flesh, and bone that our corporeal bodies are composed of are very real. But that's not what I mean when I'm describing the "self".

What I mean by the "self" is that cluster of behaviors and attitudes we use to negotiate our way through the world; the way we speak, the words we use, the way we dress, attitudes and beliefs, the way other people view us, our personalities and characteristics. This huge collection of concepts makes up what we consider to be our "selves". They are a construct, derived by a combination of genetics, upbringing, culture, and the environment and the society in which we live.

They are a construct in the same way that the

game of basketball (I could use any sport here), is a construct. The rules are devised and made up, the lines are drawn, the baskets are placed, and the time is set.

The reason it's important for you to understand that what you call your "self" is a construct, is because by understanding this, you grasp how capable you are of changing the construct, of re-ordering things, and of shedding unhelpful self-beliefs. This information is going to be extremely useful to you as you read through this book, start to go through some of the exercises, and start to feel better about yourself.

This book is about real change. It's about the science and history behind negative thoughts and beliefs and its debilitating effect on the lives of so many people. It's also about how you can change the way you feel, how you can change your negative thinking patterns and exercise real improvements in your life.

By following the simple strategies in this book, you will set yourself on a path of potentially limitless improvement, as you cast away your old, destructive self-beliefs.

This book will help you if you are racked with self-doubt, lack confidence, or feel the world is against you.

This book will partially help you if you suffer from depression. But let's get this straight. In my research for this book, I have read a number of self-help books. In at least two of them, (oddly highly rated by its reviewers), the recommendation for depression is to simply stop feeling depressed.

This is a dangerous perspective as it implies that depression is the sufferer's fault. Depression is a debilitating entity at its worst, a result of chemical and hormonal imbalances. Anybody who feels they are suffering from clinical depression should seek medical advice.

However, if you're feeling low (not the same as depression), this book can help you escape the trap of rumination, where continual self-loathing thoughts swirl around the brain. The good news is that there are things here that can help you even if you are depressed.

This book is also for you:

- if you want to make improvements in your life.

- if you want better intimate relationships with your friends and family.

- if you feel you're missing the boat in terms of financial opportunities.

- if you are struggling with your weight, or general levels of fitness.

It's for anybody really who wants to exercise some real change in their lives to achieve some of their dream goals.

My name is Max J. Harrison and I have, for many years, studied psychology. As a result, I have become an expert in communications and have published several books on the topic.

I have dealt with hundreds, if not thousands, of people, and it's my belief that the core of happiness is the truth. Understanding the truth about yourself is critical for your own self-worth and self-connection. Understanding the truth about yourself will also help you understand and empathize with the truth about other people.

I have conducted extensive research on humans and herd behavior. For those not familiar with the term "herd behavior", it indicates when a group or cluster of individuals appears to make decisions based on their peer group, or any crowd of people.

Sometimes following the herd is a good thing, but much about our communication and our actions are based on socially indoctrinated cues that don't always allow us to judge a situation objectively. We see things through the eyes of the herd. In many instances, our responses and directions are detrimental to our own health or personal well-being.

Here is my main view. When in doubt always choose yourself, instead of suffering from internal emotional issues caused by being a people pleaser. In order to choose yourself, you need to sever the link between your conditioning and your actions.

In this book, I want to take you on a journey where you choose yourself and your own instincts before following the herd. If you follow the herd I want it to only be because it is the right thing to do. There is another important concept to talk about here and that is proper selfishness.

Proper Selfishness

When I encourage you in the title of this book to "choose yourself", it may appear that what I'm advocating is a form of self-absorbed, narcissistic selfishness, but nothing could be further from the truth. It's just that many times, when people do things to follow the herd, or because they are desperately trying to please other people, they end up doing things that are not good for them at all.

They are not choosing themselves at all. What I am advocating is completely different, and can be called "proper selfishness."

The term proper selfishness was coined by the Irish philosopher and business guru, Charles Handy (Handy, 1991). To cite a brilliant example of what this term means. All you have to do is think about the last time you were on a flight. You may have been on your own, but around you will probably have seen families, some with very small, dependent children.

The advice given during the pre-flight talk from the stewards, the one which most people ignore, is that in the case of an emergency, particularly one which involves oxygen masks coming down, you need to put your own mask on first, before you take care of anybody else.

Imagine having one or two children in your charge on that flight. Imagine an emergency. Imagine those oxygen masks dropping down, masks which could mean the difference between consciousness and unconsciousness, and could mean the difference between life and death.

Your first instinct might be to go to your children and put their masks on first. But being properly selfish means that you put your own mask on first. By tending to and prioritizing your own needs first, you are now in a much stronger position to attend to the needs of people around you. You will not lose consciousness because you have a flow of oxygen in your lungs and therefore you can very quickly move to help your family and other people around you. This is probably the best example of "proper selfishness" there is.

Looking after yourself, emotionally, physically and mentally puts you in a far stronger position to interact healthily with the people you care for, and help them, if that's what they need.

So, if you think the advice to "choose yourself" advocated by this book is selfish, you're right, but it's the kind of selfishness that is positive and beneficial to other people. This is as opposed to the narcissistic, self-absorbed selfishness that we see sometimes in our society.

The other concept important in this book is the subconscious. The notion that there is an underlying thought process behind all of our actions, that is unbeknownst to us. The subconscious first found its way into the psychological arena with Sigmund Freud. The subconscious, according to Freud, underpins all of our conscious actions, and yet we appear to have no control over it.

There are other explanations for the way we think, or to be more precise, the way we respond, and we'll go through some of the more pertinent concepts later in the book.

For now, it's time to look at how our thinking, for good or bad, profoundly influences every aspect of our lives.

When in Doubt – Always Choose Yourself!

Chapter 1: The Impact of Negative Thinking, and the Radiating Goodness of Positive Thinking.

What a lovely feel-good chapter title. I can think of no other way to describe how positive thinking can radiate such a wealth of benefits to you, physically, biologically, emotionally and externally.

By externally, I mean how positive thinking can have such a beautiful effect on the relationships you have with other people, your work, your social life, and even your vocabulary. It can positively impact your responses and reactions to bad news, whether it's the bad news spewed out on a minute by minute basis by rolling 24-hour news channels, or the more personalized bad news of, for example, not getting a promotion, or being involved in a car accident. The macro (the big) and the micro (the small).

Positive thinking affects all of them. To be more

precise, positive and negative thinking affects and dictates your reaction to the events in life that don't go your way.

A negative mindset can trap you forever. The minor car accident you may have had becomes a major incident, as you panic or lose your temper. And if you don't suffer from a negative mindset and for some reason want to, feel free to pick any rolling news channel and watch it for half a day. I guarantee that if you already feel bad you will feel worse, and if you feel good when you started watching, those good feelings will be somewhat battered.

This is an important point, the way external messages can potentially have an impact on your internal moods, and in this chapter I will be discussing the impact of negative and positive feelings on people's lives.

Just where do these thoughts come from? Why do we think the way we think? And the biggest question of all, can we change the way we think? (spoiler alert - yes you can!).

What are Thoughts?

In the animal kingdom, we human beings are unique in many ways. One of the most significant differences is the manner in which we communicate - not just using rule-bound languages (apparently there are almost 6500 languages in current use in the world), but the fact that we use both audio (speech) and visual (writing) senses to communicate in those languages.

Probably the most important distinction between us and the rest of the animal kingdom is self-awareness, or rather an exquisitely developed sense of self-awareness (various levels of self-awareness can be found in other animals including apes, magpies and ravens.)

While debate rages amongst evolutionary biologists as to when homo sapiens acquired this ability, there is a general consensus that something happened around about 40,000 years ago that enabled humans to reflect on themselves. Indeed, the oldest known cave paintings featuring depictions of humans and animals, found in two regions now known as France and Indonesia, date back to just over 40000 years ago. It's hard to overstate the significance of this development to human beings.

With advanced human self-awareness came the development of empathy - the two go hand-in-hand, because inevitably an awareness of one's "self" is accompanied by an understanding of other human "selves" and how they exist independently. I would also argue that self-awareness spurred on the development of languages, religion and the creation of the concept of art.

Before self-awareness became so well-developed, humans simply existed from day to day just like most of the rest of the animal kingdom. Most non-human animals are seen as not having a particular agenda, apart from an evolutionary and biological one - primarily to eat, sleep and multiply.

While any claimed link between self-awareness and our thought processes is purely theoretical, self-awareness and thinking do seem to go hand-in-hand.

We make the mistake of believing that our thoughts are separate from our bodies. But thoughts originate from the brain, and that's where the magic occurs.

Our brain is an astonishing concoction of minuscule connections that dictate everything about us. Our thoughts, our feelings, and our actions occur thanks to an exquisitely complex relationship between our nervous system, our endocrine system (a series of glands within the body that secrete hormones.

Recent developments in neuroscience (the study of the brain), have provided us with remarkable insights into where our thought processes originate, and which parts of the brain are primarily responsible for particular actions and feelings. I stress the word "primarily" because those recent developments in neuroscience have also discovered a phenomenon called neuroplasticity. More on that later.

This is how the process of thinking generally works. The millions of nerve cells scattered around the body gather and detect information about the external world. These nerve cells, via one of our five senses (sight, smell, touch, taste and hearing) transmit information via the nervous system to the brain. It's this transmission of information that is a basic principle of how we think.

The brain itself is a maelstrom of connections over which information, in the form of electrical impulses, passes at lightning speeds. Our nerve cells detect, our brain interprets, and a thought emerges. This is a stupendous simplification, but one which holds water.

Why Do We Think the Way We Do?

While the nerve to brain link offers a brief explanation behind the physiological process of thinking, it doesn't explain why our brains interpret the information given to it in so many individual ways.

One hundred people who witness a spectacle could react and respond to it in one hundred different ways. It's the response to events which dictates our actions, feelings and emotions, whether they be negative or positive. Over the last two centuries a number of theories have evolved as to why we react the way we do. There are a couple that are of chief interest to us.

I have already mentioned the concept of the subconscious, developed by Sigmund Freud in the late 1900s. According to Freudian theory, there are two separate parts of the mind and our thinking processes, which operate independently and yet profoundly influence each other.

The first is the conscious mind; that is the part of your mind that is currently reading and interpreting these words. It's the part of your mind that makes you aware of how warm or cold you feel, the pains in your legs or other parts of the body, whether you feel sad or happy, and, of course, those specific words and sentences that we call thoughts. It is, according to the theory, the tip of the iceberg.

Because underneath it all lies the subconscious mind. It is unknown and, at least on the surface, uncontrollable. It dictates how you react to external stimuli. You may see a banana (I'm looking at one right now) and feel hungry (like I do), or it might make you laugh or cry, make you angry or sad. I'm really not making this up, but there is something called bananaphobia. It's a rare condition in which people are palpably nervous and afraid of bananas, to the point where they cannot be in the same room as one. If it sounds like I'm mocking this affliction or making light of it, I promise you I'm not.

For those people who suffer from it, it's a genuine condition, just like, for example, the fear of pansies, or feet, of the number 13, or even the fear of fear itself (phobophobia). Something unconscious, i.e. unknown, is driving that fear - something that lies in the subconscious mind.

Phobias are a useful example of how the subconscious mind can have a significant impact on people's thoughts, behaviors, and actions in their conscious minds.

Freudian psychotherapy revolves around a deep-seated and long-term analysis of where these subconscious fears come from, in order to change and address them. While the methodology and techniques of Freudian analysis have fallen out of favor in recent years, the concept of there being two dual thought processes, one that we can control and one that we have less control over dominates most theories of psychology, and is the central tenet of this book.

I am not going to discuss too much what every single school of psychology thinks about these two dual processes, but it's worth dwelling on a couple of pertinent theories that are relevant.

Psychiatry and psychotherapy are full of activity revolving around fundamentally altering the way your subconscious mind works.

For example, in transactional analysis therapy, its creator Eric Berne (1961) talked about "life scripts", which he described as a pathway through the unconscious created during our childhood experiences, and bolstered by our parents and other childhood influences. The scripts describe the way we view our lives, and temper the way we act and interact in certain situations.

According to Berne, these scripts are self-fulfilling, in that we spend our lives interpreting external stimulation and things that happen to us in a way that bolsters our views of ourselves, and confirms these life-scripts, rather than challenging those views.

The role of transactional analysis (TA) is to challenge these life scripts and write new ones, to dig up those old pathways and lay new paths, ones that lead to healthier responses.

More recently the psychologist and economist Daniel Kahneman has written a book called *Thinking Fast and Slow*. He tackles the duality of a conscious and unconscious way of thinking more from a neurological perspective.

Kahneman posits that there are two competing systems in your brain, constantly fighting over the control of your behavior and responses. This fascinating insight also shows that the brain itself will go for the most expedient option, one which requires it to do as little as possible, and therefore will jump to the quickest response, but not always the best one.

What all three of the above theories have in common is our ability to tackle our conscious thought processes and to address what lies behind them, in our unconscious thought processes.

In essence, **we can change the way we**

think. Look at those words. Read them out loud. If you have come to this book because you're unhappy with aspects of your life, take comfort from those words. You can change the way you think, and because most of our actions stem from our thinking, you can change your life.

Neuroplasticity

The idea that you can alter unconscious thought processes wasn't always accepted. Indeed, during the birth of Freudian analysis it was thought that the brain was akin to a fixed machine. And like all machines, you couldn't change it, not without screwing it up.

In this world, where the brain was an unchangeable organ, depression was a fixed thing, fear was fixed, joy was fixed. You were the way you were, and no amount of tinkering with the machinery would make much difference. Furthermore, each part of the brain had a particular and discrete function. This permeated our scientific thinking, and even our culture.

For example, think of the left brain, right brain differences toted for the last century. The theory is that the left brain is more in control of analytical methodology, while the right brain is responsible for the creative or artistic side of things. People were described as being left-brained, i.e. more methodical and analytical, or right-brained, and more creative.

But recent studies have shown this to be effectively nonsense. Neuroscientists now believe that, while parts more responsible for language development tend to be on the left side of the brain, and attention more on the right, nobody has a leaning for either way (Fuchs, 2014). This left brain- right brain theory came about because of our view of the brain as a mechanical, fixed entity.

The mechanistic view of the brain was swept away by the concept of neuroplasticity in the late 20th century, though to be fair, the term neuroplasticity was first used by the Polish scientist Jersey Konorski in the 1930s.

The principle behind neuroplasticity is that the brain is malleable. While there are parts of the brain that are more associated with particular functions (for instance, the prefrontal cortex is strongly linked to the expression of personalities, complex planning, decision making, and social behavior), these functions don't only happen within that particular part of the brain. Furthermore, if the prefrontal cortex becomes damaged or impaired in any way, it has been shown that other parts of the brain, at least to some extent, take over those functions.

Neuroplasticity has demonstrated that the brain is a far more flexible organ then virtually any other part of the body, that all of the actions within the body are interdependent of different brain parts, and in some cases other parts of the brain will, with training, learn to take over some of the functionality destroyed by brain-damaging events like a stroke.

This concept of neuroplasticity has fundamentally changed the way we view our brains. It has had an impact on treating stroke victims, the way we treat blindness or language impairment, or conditions such as ADHD. It has also fundamentally changed our view of psychotherapy; in particular, there is now an acknowledgment that we can change the way we think, because our brains do not stop learning new things, no matter how old we are.

This leads us to the exciting conclusion that whatever negative thoughts we have can be, with effort, changed and amended.

The Link Between the Subconscious and Conscious.

A few years ago, I was in a friend's back garden. They were having a barbecue. Their delightful three-year-old daughter was playing in the dirt, and having a great time. She stood up, her hands filthy and said, "Look mummy, a pider." That's how she pronounced it.

In the palm of her hand was a fairly large, harmless house spider. Her mummy, who had been preoccupied, looked over, immediately ran to her daughter, slapped the spider off her hand and stamped violently on it. "Be careful!" she shouted.

Her daughter burst into tears. Let's get one thing clear, I'm not criticizing the mother's behavior. She reacted instinctively. Spiders look scary. It's even said that we are evolutionarily programed to recoil in the presence of spider

Five years later the daughter, now eight years old, is petrified of spiders, and if there is one in her bedroom she screams until it is dealt with.

Is it too simplistic to say that her attitude towards spiders was informed solely by what happened in the garden that day? Possibly, but until that day that three-year-old child never had a problem with spiders. However, she did now, to the point where you would call it full-blown arachnophobia.

"They f**k you up, your mum and dad,

They may not mean to, but they do.

They fill you with the faults they had

And add some extra just for you."

Excerpt from This be the Verse by Phillip Larkin. **(Larkin, 2001.)**

What Philip Larkin's poem alludes to, and what the story of the spider also demonstrates, is the fundamental influence our parents have over us in our childhood. To be more precise, it is primarily in our childhood where our foibles and fears and views of ourselves, are forged and molded by the people around us.

Of course, this is mainly our parents. But it's not just parents - our siblings, extended relatives, babysitters and nannies, the lady in the shop who always had a kind word for children, the miserable teacher, our friends, society as a whole, what we watch, what we read, what we hear and see, all of these factors have the capacity to fundamentally influence the attitude of our unconscious mind, or as Freud called it, the subconscious. (To be consistent, for the rest of this book I will now refer to the unconscious mind as the subconscious.)

It is in these formative years where children may hear a lot of negative phrases such as:-

- You clumsy oaf!

- You naughty little boy/girl!

- No, don't do that. Why? Because I said so, that's why.

- You're doing it wrong, I'll show you.

- Why are you always crying?

- Do what you're told.

- What is wrong with you?

- You'll always be naughty/stupid.

- Come on, stop crying.

- I'll just leave you here then.

- Get out, leave me alone.

- You're so ungrateful.

- Well done, but why can't you do this all the time?

- Stop being annoying.

- Don't eat that, you'll get fat.

- I'm so fat. Time to start dieting.

- It's not a big deal.

- Calm down!

- You're too lazy!

- Hurry up, we're going to be late!

- Why do I have to keep telling you?

- You're being ridiculous.

- I'm disappointed in you.

- Your sister could do it, why can't you?

- You make me feel sad.

- You'd better do what I say or there'll be trouble.

- You ought to be ashamed.

- Don't be mad at your sister, she didn't mean it.

I'm not saying that every child is subject to the kinds of comments listed here all the time. But some are. Many hear them sometimes. I know I was exposed to some of these sentences over the years.

Imagine hearing these phrases every day, week, or even every month, over a 10 - 15 year period. That constant drip-drip-drip of criticism, particularly at a very young age, embeds into the child's subconscious, and digs its claws in good and tight. If a child is told he's clumsy enough times, he believes it - and carries that belief in his subconscious through to his adult years.

Judith, somebody I worked with, told me about her father, a very strict man. In her fifties now, she recalled how full of fun and laughter her house was when the father was at work, but an hour before he was due back, the house went quiet as they waited pensively for the self-styled master of the house to return.

She never knew what mood he was going to be in. Well, she knew he was going to be in a bad mood but what she didn't know was who was going to receive the full brunt of his anger. Sometimes it was her mother, other times it was her sister or brother. Many times it was her, and her Father would gather all the family in one room to publicly berate her, to tell her she was a disappointment, to criticize her schoolwork or the way she looked. Once, when she was eight years old he said to her, "Why don't you go and throw yourself in the river? Nobody would miss you."

Fear. That's what she felt when he was in the house. Her childhood was punctuated by daily bouts of fear and humiliation. Now, 40 years have passed and yet she tells me she still feels the fear. She has never really got away from it.

So far, I have recounted two stories, Judith's, and the three-year-old girl with a spider. Whatever happens in our childhood gets translated and embedded into our subconscious. From a Transactional Analysis perspective, they are turned into life scripts, written deeply into the subconscious.

The subconscious mind acts as a huge memory storage facility, which records everything that happens to you. While it sounds a bit like the memory of a computer, the subconscious differs greatly in the way those memories are recalled. If you have a file on your computer and you call it up you know that the file is going to be identical to the one you saved, and that when you open it again and again, without any changes, it will be identical. By contrast, the subconscious filters and interprets our memories.

At an early age the subconscious is, for the want of a better word, programed. The programs are your external environment, your parents, et cetera. Whatever they feed into your mind sticks. And the more potent the memory, the more repeated the behavior is, and the more solidified your programming becomes.

Let's take the example of spider girl. What happened in the garden with her mother was a one-off event but to that three-year-old girl, not used to seeing her mother frightened or annoyed, it was a huge occurrence. That event magnified itself in her subconscious and became part of her programming.

How Negative Feelings Hurt You

Let me define what I mean by negative thinking. I'm lumping in feelings of fear, of being threatened, of feeling inferior, of anxiety and panic. I'm including feelings of sadness, of worry and all the other words that have negative connotations.

Let me just single out for a second feelings of fear, panic and being threatened. Over the last few centuries and millennia, these feelings have evolved in order to allow us to respond as quickly as we can to threats to our safety. In situations where we are under threat, the fight or flight response kicks in. It's the response where we either fight back or flee during a threatening situation.

These emotions have served us well, especially in the days when we were hunter/gatherers, and there were threats from other animals and human beings. It still serves us well now, in extreme circumstances.

But this fight or flight response also kicks in if we are worried about something, or anxious, for example when you are having a heated discussion at work with a colleague, or you're struggling to finish a project and the deadline is looming. Our brains and our subconscious are wired to respond to negative thoughts and feelings in the same fight or flight mode as if we were being physically attacked.

In these everyday instances, the fight or flight response does not help. Any form of negative thinking can trigger psychological stress, and it wreaks havoc on our bodies, let alone our emotional states.

In a recent study, subjects were required to sort things into two categories. Those people who reported that they worried or felt negative thoughts over 50% of the time showed a significant impairment in their ability to sort objects, particularly as the difficulty of the sorting task increased. When the brain has to negotiate complex tasks, negative thoughts impair your ability to process the information in front of you, and to think clearly about what you need to do. In short, negative thinking prevents you from solving problems (Komninnos, 2017).

Recent developments in neuroscience have discovered that negative thoughts and feelings are stored in a part of the brain called the amygdala, which is also primarily responsible for their brain's fight or flight response. So, when faced with an everyday situation, for instance being stuck in traffic, an average person will decide that the level of threat to their safety is minimal and that the most important thing is the annoyance of it. They are, therefore, able to relax through it until the traffic clears.

By contrast, somebody who experiences high levels of stress continually thinks negative thoughts continually, or somebody suffering from PTSD, responds as if the traffic is a threat. The ability to differentiate between a real threat and merely an annoyance is blurred.

Another part of the brain, the thalamus cannot distinguish between negative thoughts and actual danger. And that is why negative thoughts make the thalamus get you ready to flee.

It's a bizarre and discomforting experience, sitting quietly in a room, suddenly sensing that your heart rate has increased, your breathing is shallow, you have started to sweat, and your blood pressure is elevated. You wonder why when there appears to be no rational reason. But negative thoughts prepare your body for an attack. That's why you feel so bad, because they trigger a stress response.

It's not just feeling bad at the time either. These things take some time to subside and, over the long-term, negative thinking induced stress can change the brain and increase the likelihood of disorders such as depression, anxiety, bipolar disorder, and ADHD.

At worst, continually thinking negative thoughts and therefore triggering tremendous stress responses is the equivalent of having post-traumatic stress disorder. Such chronic stress affects both your mood and your memories. The brain, the most complex structure in the universe, is brilliant at learning lessons from bad experiences but is often not very good at differentiating between those bad experiences.

So far, I have talked about the biological impact, in particular on the brain, of negative thinking. I haven't even touched upon the impact on people's lifestyles. In my experience, negative thinking and negative views about oneself have probably prevented millions of people in the world from realizing their true potential.

It has blighted their relationships, their jobs, their fitness, their weight, and it has increased levels of depression and other emotional disorders. It is a self-fulfilling prophecy. You feel crap about yourself and something happens, which confirms why you feel crap about yourself, and so you feel even more crap about yourself. The damage negative thinking does to people all over the world is almost incalculable.

Within the brain, there exists a complex network comprising of neurons, billions of them, and electrochemical switches called neurotransmitters. The neurons and transmitters form an intricate communications network, transmitting messages to and from every part of the brain. When these messages are received the specific part of the brain responds as it is programed to, and incredibly small but incredibly powerful chemical substances (hormones) are sent to our brain, our central nervous system, and to our bodies. These chemicals control everything we do and feel.

So, every thought we have is translated into a series of electrical impulses, and these electrical impulses, in turn, dictate which chemicals or hormones are released into the bloodstream - these in turn influence what you do and how you feel.

Therefore, your thoughts, which come from your pre-programed subconscious are affecting you. In fact, they are controlling your responses. Negative thoughts incite negative, unhealthy responses.

The good news is it is possible to replace negative thoughts with positive ones.

Neuroscientist Dr. Rick Hanson, creator of a brain training program designed to improve your happiness declares that the people who completed a training program designed to replace negative thoughts with positive ones "experience significantly less anxiety and depression, and significantly greater self-control, savoring, compassion, love, contentment, joy, gratitude, self-esteem, self-compassion, satisfaction with life, and overall happiness."(Hanson, 2019).

There's a lot at stake here. All of those negative thoughts that have been holding you back and affecting your health can be reduced, and even replaced, with effort. It is possible to retrain and reprogram your subconscious mind.

I'm not saying it will be easy. The actions and activities I outline in the rest of this book are relatively straightforward and easy to do, but you are trying to replace a program etched into your subconscious and dictating your actions for years. You are replacing ancient patterns and repaving them with new, more positive thoughts. If you are prepared to put the work in, the opportunities for you to achieve your goals are potentially limitless.

As an independent author with a small marketing budget, reviews are my livelihood on this platform.

If you are enjoying this book I would appreciate it if you left me your honest feedback.

I love hearing from my readers and I personally read every single review.

Sincerely Yours, Max J. Harrison

Chapter 2: How To Recognize Your Own Negative Thoughts Patterns and behavior

Negative thought patterns are not as easy to recognize as you might think. There are some extremely obvious examples, for instance, if you catch yourself looking in a mirror and calling yourself a loser, or scrutinizing your body and picking out all its faults, these appear to be fairly obvious.

But sometimes negative thoughts have become so ingrained in you that you may not even recognize them for what they are. Your negative thoughts seem like a normal response.

In addition, some of your responses and behaviors are not necessarily triggered by an overt thought, but just might be so embedded in you that you respond negatively in an automatic way.

There are ways and means of spotting this negative behavior, whether you're aware of it or not, and in this chapter, we'll go through the process and get you on the road to some practical exercises.

Those Pesky ANTs

There's a name for the kind of unconscious negative thinking. That name is "automatic negative thoughts" (ANTs).

These ANTs are different for each person, making them unique, specific and a little harder to spot. Furthermore, they emerge spontaneously and appear without you even being aware that they're there. This makes it harder to identify them as a negative thought because they may just be so steeped into your subconscious you don't question them.

Happily, there is a psychological technique called mindfulness that plays a pivotal role in identifying these ANTs, letting them go, and replacing them with other, more positive thoughts.

Mindfulness.

Mindfulness, and in particular mindfulness meditation, became popular buzzwords towards the end of the 20th century, the beginning of the 21st.

Mindfulness is the act of paying close conscious attention to all the thoughts, feelings and emotions cascading through your mind at a particular point in time. Importantly, it is a way of studying these feelings and thoughts without being critical of them or judging them.

It's a way of being fully aware of what's happening in your present moment without being bogged down by what's happened in your past or being concerned about the future. Some people confuse it with the phrase 'living for the moment', but that glib cliché doesn't apply here. It's more about living IN a particular and brief moment.

Imagine those three thousand plus thoughts crashing through your brain every hour. I like to think of those thoughts as being like the detritus picked up by a huge hurricane swirling around you.

It's hard to focus on any particular point, but then one thought looms in front of you; it could be about anything, so you focus on it. It may be a thought that makes you angry, afraid or sad. But with a mindful approach, what you are able to do is scrutinize the thought without being judgmental, without reproach, and with kindness towards yourself.

The very act of taking a step back from the thought and scrutinizing it calmly is sometimes enough to break the cycle of angry or sad rumination these thoughts can kick-off. They become far easier to let go. Particularly in the case of ANTs, a mindful look at how you're thinking and where those thoughts come from is extremely useful. It enables you to recognize them, and be aware of those negative thoughts the next time they pass by. They stop being quite so automatic.

The mindfulness technique of looking at your thoughts impartially and non-judgmentally is incredibly useful, but then you have to come crashing back down to Earth.

If you decide that the thought is not healthy to you, then you can start the process of letting it go and replacing it with more positive thoughts. But you have to make a judgment about it in the first place in order to do that. To make that judgment you need to step out of a non-judgmental mindfulness mode. The process of reframing your negative thoughts and replacing them with more positive and realistic ones is covered in more detail in chapters seven and eight of this book, "Journaling" and "Positive Affirmations".

Types of ANTs

Even with mindfulness techniques, identifying ANTs can be difficult, so here is a list of the most common:

Blown up thoughts or thoughts made small.

This is where people give more weight to something negative that happens to them in their life and tend to trivialize or make less important the positive things to happen.

At its most extreme, the tendency to trivialize one's abilities and positive experiences and magnify negative ones can lead to something called impostor syndrome, a psychological pattern in which an individual doubts his or her achievements and has a persistent internalized fear of being exposed as a fraud.

On a more mundane level, if somebody congratulates you on something you have done, and you dismiss their praise because they don't know enough about you, or because they got it wrong, this is one of your ANTs.

Binary or black-and-white thinking.

Perhaps you're writing a book, and somebody questioned you about one of your sentences. A binary or black-and-white thought will identify the entire book as rubbish and will encourage the thinker to give it up straight away.

For black-and-white thinkers, things are either perfect or flawed, good or bad, successes or failures. An individual who suffers from this black-and-white thinking finds it difficult to accept that there are shades of grey between the black and the white, or the perfect or flawed. This is one of the most common ANTs.

Jumping to the wrong conclusions

This is where an individual judge's something to be a certain way without having enough proof or evidence to support their conclusions. You're walking down the corridor, and you pass your boss, but he doesn't say hello. You start worrying that you've done something wrong and that your boss disapproves of you. There is simply no evidence to support this. You could just as easily jump to the conclusion that the boss needs glasses, or has had no sleep, or has an upset tummy.

Overgeneralization.

This is where we draw faulty conclusions about something based on just one example. For example, you may apply for a job and be unsuccessful, and then overgeneralize and say that as a result of this you will never get a job.

Mind reading

This is where an individual thinks that others will react badly to something that he or she does or says without having proof that it's a possibility.

Should or must statements

This is a feeling that you or everyone else has to act in a certain way and when things don't happen as you think they should, it makes you feel bad.

Personalization

This applies when you believe that the actions of other people are a kind of direct personal reaction to you. A person who experiences this train of thinking has a tendency to compare themselves to others, usually negatively.

To understand the debilitating impact of a combination of ANTs let's use an example.

A colleague at work might come up to you and say: I just wanted to tell you I liked your idea at the meeting today, although I could also see that you were a bit nervous when you were telling people about it.

Your reaction might be to think "everybody saw how nervous I was, I'm a disaster, I always do it wrong, that's the last time I put myself forward in a meeting again."

We can see a number of ANTs kicking in here. We can see the blowing up of the issue and the trivializing of the good points, we can see black and white thinking, "I'm a disaster", and we can see the jumping to conclusions without having enough evidence.

While these ANTSs are not easy to recognize, it is worth putting the effort of scrutinizing every response that you have, to notice how your mind takes a molehill and turns it into Mount Everest. Being aware of all your negative thought patterns is a fundamental step when attempting to control and replace your negative thoughts.

Other Types of Negative Thoughts and How to Recognize Them.

There is a huge range of specific negative thoughts that you can think of. I'm clumsy, I'll never finish this course, look at how fat I am, I'll never attract a mate, I'm not attractive enough. Truly, I could go on forever listing the ways in which we torture ourselves. But they can be categorized into a few broad categories not yet mentioned.

Negative self-labeling

This is one of the most common and include phrases such as, "I'm a failure", "I'm not good enough", "If people knew what I was really like they wouldn't want to know me", "I'm useless", "I'm a loser", "I'm rubbish at XY or Z."

As common as these labels are, they are quite easy to recognize.

Catastrophizing

"I can't believe I'm stuck in traffic, I'm going to be late and that meeting starts bang on nine. My boss is going to be furious. She'll have strong words with me, or worse, give me a warning, or worse, fire me. What will I do then? I'll have no money. How would I afford the place I live in? And how will I get another job? I've been off the market for years, I'm rubbish at interviews at the best of times, and my skills are so out of date. Maybe I should just turn around and crawl back into bed. I wish I could."

When you read the above scenario it's almost comical, isn't it? How does somebody go from being stuck in traffic to losing her job and having nowhere to live? Step-by-step, one catastrophe leads to a worse catastrophe, leads to a worse catastrophe, and so on.

For the people locked into this kind of response, it's anything but funny. And the above scenario is a recanting from an acquaintance, Betsy. This is how she sometimes perceives herself. Interestingly, when she got into work she was the first there because everybody else was coming in the same direction, and they got stuck in the same traffic! That should've made her feel better, but it didn't, it just led to a bout of self-flagellation concerning how she overreacted so ridiculously, and made herself feel upset.

Desperate need for approval.

So many people try hard to be people pleasers. Their own happiness is contingent on whether other people like them. People pleasers like this also have a tendency to assume that if somebody is upset it's their fault.

Attempting to be a people pleaser all the time is a lose-lose scenario. Firstly, it is literally impossible to please everybody all the time. Somebody will be upset at something that you do in life. Secondly, trying to please people all the time may put you in a position where you're not happy with yourself. The boss comes and asks you to do a rush job. You were going to go out tonight and see that movie you fancy. But you say okay, and you think, "I'll do it to please him".

Rational thinking would have allowed you to see that saying, "No, I can't do it right now, I have plans tonight, but I'll do it first thing in the morning", would have had a minimal impact on your standing with your boss. But rational thinking usually takes a backseat in situations like this, which is why you need the power of positive thinking.

Ignoring the present.

There are people who find it hard to relax, who think relaxation is something for the future, when you've finished all your tasks. Trouble is, the tasks never finish. This kind of mentality is both overtly self-destructive and subtly negative. It implies that you are only allowed to have a rest when you deserve it, by finishing your endless list of jobs.

Focusing on pain.

The logic here is this: "If I dwell on my unhappiness, and what went wrong, maybe I'll feel better."

The trouble is you don't feel better. Dwelling on your negative thoughts turns into a destructive bout of rumination. Rumination is where you consider something over and over, almost like a record stuck in a groove. And rumination is one of the first symptoms of depression.

Negative Self-Talk versus Thinking about Something Bad.

I've already used the term "negative self-talk" several times in this book. It's high time for a fuller explanation of this term.

Negative self-talk is an amalgam of all the bad things you think, feel, or say about yourself. You may not be literally talking to yourself, though many people do this as well. I've witnessed colleagues at work drop some papers and shout out loud "Idiot!". That's a graphic example of negative self-talk.

Mostly, it refers to the noise in your head, one of

the 3000 plus thoughts swirling around your consciousness every hour. And of course, there are the ANTs as well, and sometimes not even words, just bad feelings. These insidious feelings are a much more subtle form of self-talk, but self-talk nonetheless.

But you know what? It's okay to feel bad about things. It's okay to feel sad, angry or afraid. If your favorite football team loses by one point, it's okay to feel annoyed. If you hear that a friend you haven't seen for a while has died, of course, it's okay to feel sad.

Our feelings are outlets, and play a vital role in our everyday lives. There's a big difference, however, in thinking these naturally downbeat thoughts, and dealing with the constant stream of negative put-downs that pop-up from your subconscious and make you feel bad.

It's okay to feel bad about your football team losing, but if you want to attribute that loss to the fact that you forgot to wear your lucky shirt on game day, as if somehow their loss is your fault, that's negative self-talk.

Let's say you lose your job, a common scenario. It's okay to feel bad, to feel disappointed that it happened, to feel some anxiety about paying your bills or getting another job. These responses and feelings exist in order to help you process what is important to you, and to work on what to do about them.

The next day or week you start looking for new work, polishing up your resume, phoning around your contacts, temporarily deferring your bills; those feelings of natural anxiety have helped galvanize you into taking the action you need.

If, however, you not only have these naturally bad feelings but then blame yourself, class yourself as a failure, become so agitated and stressed that you can't seem to take any remedial action to find another job, that's when your negative self-talk is bashing you around the face, holding you back, paralyzing you. See the difference.

The summary of this section is this: Don't feel bad about feeling bad. The feelings you have are a result of faulty programming. But nobody programed you deliberately. The parents who put you down in certain circumstances were probably put down themselves in turn and therefore learned that this was the way to act, the way to be.

For almost all of the rest of the book, we are going to talk about strategies to get you out of this funk and start living the life you deserve.

How to Recognize Negative Thoughts.

There's a big difference between hearing something and listening to something. If you're in bed in the middle of the night and you hear a noise downstairs, you sit up in bed and you suddenly start listening. Better terms for these are passive listening and active listening.

I am currently in a coffee house writing this section of the book. There's a lot of noise in the background, of clinking cups and conversation. I can hear it, but I am not actively listening to it.

For two minutes I have actively listened, really focused on what's going on. I now know that for the third day running the shop has had a problem with the coffee machine, and the lady two tables away from me is going to ask her boss for a raise when he gets back from her vacation in Cancun.

Now let's take this analogy of active and passive listening to the swirl of thoughts cascading around your brain. Of course, you can't actively "listen" but what you can do instead is actively pay attention to what these thoughts are saying.

What you're trying to do here is identify the commentary and themes of your inner critic, the voice that is fed by the programming within your subconscious.

It's always there and it's always chattering away, but usually, you don't pay too much attention to it, even though it has a profound effect on your thoughts, actions, and feelings. By taking a pause and considering what's being said, you're going to learn about your main negative thoughts and your main negative patterns of behavior.

On the whole, your inner critic is often wrong. Some people are lucky enough to have inner voices that are supportive and realistic. But for many people, particularly those who experience episodes of sadness or depression their head-chatter is usually profoundly negative. There are some (not many) instances where that head-chatter needs to be negative.

For example, if you're just about to get into a car and start driving it, and you don't really know how to drive, it's perfectly acceptable for your inner critic to scream at you, "Don't do it!"

Usually though, your negative self-talk is wrong, to your cost. So, recognizing that your inner self-talk is often inaccurate and wrong is a great start. Don't just accept it at face value. In a way, you've already started partially practicing mindfulness by taking pause and scrutinizing your thoughts. However, in the end, it's important to eventually not let go, but to pin each thought down and examine it under a bright, honest light. We will get to that part of the process, I promise.

Be aware of your feelings, and use those as the jumping-off point to scrutinize your inner self-talk. When you feel annoyed or sad, depressed, angry, panicky, anxious, stressed out, guilty, afraid, discouraged, despairing or frustrated, or any other negative feelings, this is the opportunity to take a pause and interrogate your inner critic.

What is it saying about you? How does it make you feel? By concentrating on what you're feeling, and paying close attention to what your inner critic is telling you about yourself, you are well on the road to identifying the main themes of your negative self-talk, and therefore well on the road to doing something about it.

Now you have an opportunity to recognize the different forms of negative self-talk already outlined in this book, it is worthwhile to briefly recap. See if you can work out whether you are personalizing, catastrophizing, filtering out the good and concentrating on the bad, indulging in black-and-white or binary thinking, thinking self-limiting thoughts, jumping to conclusions, and all the other forms negative self-talk can take.

I have already said that most self-talk is not literally verbalized talking, but you can learn a lot by examining your speech. Try and catch yourself verbalizing, even under your breath. If you say these words, you believe them - those verbalized tics (stupid idiot!) are your inner critic taking over your vocal cords and telling its truth.

In Transactional Allowance Therapy, Eric Berne talked about life scripts as personal beliefs and how people look for things that happened to confirm and bolster their life scripts. If you believe you're stupid and say it out loud enough times or think it enough times you'll merely be looking for events in your life that confirm it, thus solidifying and strengthening your subconscious programming, your life scripts (Berne, 1961).

Also, stop yourself when you hear the words "should" or "shouldn't" in your vocabulary (when referring to yourself). These words carry with them inbuilt self-criticism.

Stop Those Negative Thoughts in Their Tracks

Find your triggers. There will be certain events in your life that encourage your negative self-talk to emerge. It could be a presentation at work, or seeing your in-laws. It could be a social evening, an appraisal, or it could even be opening emails. By finding these negative triggers you will be more aware and prepared once you start undertaking these actions.

Practice mindfulness. This is where mindfulness really helps. If you find yourself trapped on the negative self-talk train, take a pause, acknowledge the negative thought, view it kindly, impassively, accept that it is just a thought and, well, let it go. Picture it in your mind encased in a bubble, and imagine that bubble floating away. Say goodbye to it. Just by taking a pause and impartially acknowledging your negative thought as just one of 3000 thoughts per hour, you can already make an immediate difference.

Think of something specific in your mind. If you find the mindfulness technique above difficult, another thing to do is to focus on something you're familiar with and imagine yourself doing that. For instance, you could imagine yourself shopping, literally going to the shelves of your favorite store and picking up each item. Imagine yourself looking at it before putting it in your trolley, and moving on to the next item.

Or imagine changing a tire. Literally visualize yourself going through the step-by-step process of reviewing the faulty tire, going to the trunk of your car, lifting up the covers, picking up the tire, and so on. Get into the detail, imagine you can feel the sensation of those nuts as you unscrew them.

I've used two examples that require step-by-step actions you can picture in sequence. It could be anything like this. With practice, before very long, you will find the negative thought has disappeared, defeated by your specific thinking, and you can move on with your day.

Avoid negative influencers. We all know them, people trapped in their own negative self-talk, only these people have no problem articulating their own negative thoughts and spewing them on to you. They can't help raining on your parade and making you feel bad. Are they friends? Probably not. They're best avoided. I know that sounds harsh since they are people in just as much pain as you. So, there is another way.

A famous comic who shall remain nameless told me that when he told his mother he was going to be a stand-up comic she said, "Now, why in the name of Jesus do you want to do a stupid thing like that?"

Very wisely he stopped talking to her about it, and now that he has achieved some fame his mother is incredibly proud of him. He reminded her of her first reaction, and she claimed to have no recollection of saying those words!

Our comic did the right thing. Naturally, he couldn't stop seeing his mother, but he avoided the subject of his comedy because he knew she would be constantly negative about it. He didn't avoid the negative person but successfully avoided the subject, and the opportunity for her to bring him down. You can try this with your friend who veers towards the negative. Avoid the subjects that are their trigger points, and, if they become negative, try and change the subject. If this doesn't work, make your excuses. Be properly selfish and look after yourself.

Don't try and suppress your negative thoughts. If you try to ignore them and push them away they'll come back and bite you even harder. Try making an effort to NOT think of something for one minute. It could be anything, a gorilla, your favorite meal, or the color red. After two minutes, you'll realize how hard it is.

Mindfully acknowledging those thoughts and letting them go works for many people, as already mentioned. Acknowledging those thoughts but distracting yourself by thinking of a specific step-by-step task has is also a better way. You've gently nudged the thought away, but you know it's there. Retraining your negative self-talk so that these thoughts occur less and less, and are replaced by positive self-talk, is the next logical step. The first step is to go into interrogation mode.

Question those Negative Thoughts. Questions are brilliant, because they stop you from ruminating on your negative thoughts and really get you to apply your cognitive, conscious thinking into re-examining those thoughts. Posing a well-considered question is like shining a light in a dark place.

One of the best questions you can ask yourself is this: Is this negative self-talk serving me? By simply asking that question, in many cases, the negative thoughts disappear, or at least weaken. Another good one is: How else can I look at the situation?

What would a neutral observer (if you know and trust somebody use their name in this question) think about this line of thought? If you're worried or catastrophizing, ask: What's the worst thing that can happen to me? and follow that with: Am I able to handle the worst? or: How would I handle the worst? There are hundreds of questions you could ask, but you know the best way to question yourself because the negative self-talk belongs to you.

Asking questions is the start of a process that potentially could completely reprogram your subconscious, and rewrite your life scripts. It's now time to provide you with some techniques and practices to help you to do just that.

Chapter 3: Changing Your Mindset

We've discussed where negative thoughts come from. We've discussed techniques to nip those negative thoughts in the bud. The rest of this book is about turning around your negative self-talk and converting it to at best positive helpful, or, at worst, neutral self-talk.

What is a Mindset?

A person's mindset refers to the continual, regular, and established attitudes held by them. It's the way a person thinks, and the way their opinions are formed. It's that collection of beliefs and thoughts that make up a mental attitude. A person's mindset is pivotal in influencing the way he or she responds to any given situation.

There are many mindsets people can adopt but recently Stanford University's Carol Dweck has done some fantastic work on distinguishing between two overarching mindsets that all others fall into. One is called a fixed mindset and the other, a growth mindset (Gotter, 2018).

Characteristics of a Person with a Fixed Mindset.

Is this you?

- You stick with what you know.
- You tend to think you're either good or bad at something. Therefore, inborn talent dictates how successful you will be, no matter how hard you work at something.
- You tend to focus on appearances, on how things look to other people, instead of learning and training yourself.
- You give up easily.
- You find failure humiliating. You are afraid of it.
- You will rarely try any new challenges because of your fear of failure, and how it would make you look to other people, and feel about yourself.
- You feel threatened and envious of others.
- You never developed into your full potential because you're afraid to.
- You tend to think poorly of yourself and feel it's a waste of time to

develop things because you're so bad at them. What's the point?

Characteristics of a growth mindset

Is this you?

- You can believe you can do almost anything if you put your mind and effort into it.

- You have a strong desire to learn.

- You're not afraid of a challenge.

- You don't get put off by making mistakes. Rather, you see them as opportunities to learn.

- You actually enjoy continually learning new things.

- While you do sometimes have negative thoughts, you recognize them for what they are.

- Generally, you view each situation pragmatically and honestly.

Luckily, this psychological model isn't binary. You can have a fixed mindset in some areas, and a growth mindset in others. But generally, people lean towards one or the other.

Unsurprisingly, those with a fixed mindset have a greater tendency for negative self-talk and a negative view of their own abilities. For example, if they do try something new and it goes wrong, they will catastrophize the nature of the mistake and its consequences, and will magnify the significance of the mistake, regarding themselves as complete failures. Finally, they will indulge in a little bit of black-and-white thinking: "I am no good at XYZ and therefore I am no good at anything."

But mindsets are just an amalgam of your deeply buried subconscious beliefs. Therefore, with effort, you can change them. You could adopt more of a growth mindset than a fixed one.

A fixed mindset person believes that we have innate abilities and can't change them, that intelligence is fixed, our abilities are fixed and there is no point in trying to learn anything new. As we've already discussed, with neuroplasticity this is simply not the case. Our brains can grow and learn no matter what age a person is.

A fixed mindset is the ultimate negative self-talk because, according to science, it's simply not true.

How to recognize your mindset

Regardless of whether you use the labels fixed or

growth, you need to establish what kind of mindset you have, and whether it's helping you fulfil your life's ambitions or hamper them.

So, get a pen and paper, or a new document on your computer. Write down and answer honestly the following questions:

- Do I believe my intelligence is fixed and I can't change it?
- Am I capable of learning new things?
- Am I learning new things, and do I enjoy learning new things?
- Do I believe I'm capable of much more?
- If so, am I doing anything about this belief?

These five questions will set you on the right track for establishing whether you have a growth or a fixed mindset. But you don't want to leave it there. You need to establish some more detail about the specifics of your mindset because it's an amalgam of your attitudes and beliefs.

The next step is to ask yourself if you have any achievements, aspirations, or dreams. Write them down. What are they? What did they revolve around? What mindset would you need to achieve those dreams? Let's say you left school with few qualifications, but you love the idea of being a teacher.

You could investigate exactly what you need to do to achieve this goal. What qualifications do you need? How long would it take to get them? How much work would you have to do? How could you fit it into other commitments? Would you need help? If so, who could help you?

Then, when you've got a list of actions that you would need to take to make it, you can easily identify the kind of mindset you need.

I'm not just talking about growth versus fixed mindset. If you need to earn qualifications to achieve your dream, then it's safe to say you would need a growth mindset. I'm talking about what lies underneath that, what kind of approach you would need, and what kind of qualities. Here's a list I've compiled from the above example of wanting to be a teacher.

- You would need persistence because you're going to have to study for quite a long time.
- You would need not to be put off by varying demands because you're going to have to fit it in with your current lifestyle.

- You would need to be able to make mistakes and learn from them and keep going because studying can be hard.
- You would need the ability and strength to approach people to help you, either in the work that you're r learning or to help you with your other commitments.
- You would need to keep your eyes on the prize.
- You would need to be organized.

So now you have a list of qualities that make up a mindset. Persistence, flexibility, patience, resilience, can-do attitude, et cetera, et cetera. It's a great list; don't be intimidated by it, you've got it covered.

Next step. Really listen to your inner self-talk, pay heed to your inner critic. You really need to understand what your current mindset is.

I repeat, it's not just about the difference between a growth and a fixed mindset. You may genuinely believe that it is possible to learn new things, but you also might be afraid that you personally can't do it because you're not resilient enough. You've got a combination of a growth and a fixed mindset there, but it's the belief that you can't do it, the fixed aspect of your mindset, that could hold you back from achieving your dreams.

In this process, you need to be as honest and yet as non-judgmental with yourself as you can be. Be kind to yourself. If you find out that you are afraid of failing and think you will fail all the time, that's ok. The more you articulate your own fears and your own negative self-talk, the greater the opportunities lie ahead to address it and amend or replace it.

At the end of the process, where you have paid close attention to your inner critic you may have a cluster of words that look something like this:

- Afraid of failing.

- Perceive that I will fail at everything.

- Clumsy.

- Forgetful.

- Weight conscious.

- I think I'm unattractive.

- People find me boring.

- Afraid of change.

So now you've got a list of words for the qualities

you need to display, and a list of feelings that could hold you back. The next step is to bridge the gap between these two lists. Let's summarize this entire thing.

Step one. Identify your ambitions, aspirations and dreams. Identify what you really want to do in life.

Step two. Think about your aspirations and where you are now. Come up with a list of words to identify the mindset and attitude you would need to carry to make achieving your dreams easier.

Step three. Listen closely to your inner self-talk. Come up with a list of words that identify your current mindset and attitude.

Step four. Compare and contrast the mindset you need to achieve your dreams and the mindset you currently have, and identify the gaps.

In the next few chapters, we are going to discuss in detail some of the truly life-changing steps you can take to reprogram your subconscious and get rid of the negative self-talk. We are going to be discussing positive self-talk, also known as affirmations, the benefits, and joys of journaling, the importance of establishing a productive routine in your life, and how to stay motivated.

But before we do that it's worthwhile exploring how to deal with challenging situations right now.

Challenging situations

David had a dilemma. He managed a call center of 100 people. He was popular with his managers and also with the people who worked for him. He worked hard at cultivating this because he liked to be liked. Then one day his boss delivered a bombshell. They were slicing the workforce into two separate departments and two separate locations. What that meant was that he needed to make 50 members of his team redundant.

David had never done anything like this before and he admitted to me that he had many sleepless nights. How was he going to deal with the two potentially competing concepts of being popular with his workforce and firing half of them?

David's situation feels big to him. For other people an equally big challenge might be going to the shops, or dealing with an aggressive relative. For each situation, no matter what, the following rules will help.

Rule One. Articulate, understand, and acknowledge the situation. Don't bury your head in the sand or try and stay in denial. By understanding exactly what's ahead of you can then take the appropriate actions.

Rule Two. Come up with a plan. You can either do this on your own, or enlist help. If you're doing it on your own, one way I plan is by setting a timer for three minutes and speaking into the recorder on my phone as quickly as I can, coming up with as many ways as possible to deal with the situation.

If I come up with a load of ideas and I have more, I reset the timer, and only stop when I've run out of ideas. If you try this technique, don't worry about what you say, nobody else will hear it. Don't dismiss anything. If an idea pops into your head say it. If you think it's stupid, that's just your inner critic chiming in. In this case, it's perfectly ok to ignore him. Don't worry about repeating yourself either.

Once you've finished recording, listen back and write all the ideas down. Categorize them with the most effective ideas at the top and the least effective at the bottom.

Rule Three. Don't be afraid to ask for help if you feel you need it.

Rule Four. Identify what you can change, and change it. If, for example, you worry about going to the shops because at certain times they are busy and you don't like crowds, go at a quieter time.

Rule Five. Identify and accept the things you cannot change.

Rule six. Take care of yourself during this difficult time. If you know you're going to be feeling bad or sad or angry or whatever, acknowledge it and prepare to deal with those feelings. Bolster your ability to cope by living a healthy lifestyle, getting enough sleep, exercising and eating healthily. Find ways to deal with the worst feelings. For example, go and see a movie, spend time with your loved ones, or participate in fun activities

Rule seven. Focus on the positives of your situation. Out of adversity, good things can arise. You may learn a lesson, you may even gain something. At the very least, everything you do will be a learning experience that will help you cope with similar situations in later life.

Let's go back to Dave now and his redundancy situation. After a few days of deep reflection where he even contemplated resigning, he figured that even if he did resign somebody else would make the staff redundant anyway. He also worked out that he was probably the best person to do it, because he knew them all and could soften the blow by, for example, taking steps to help them look for other jobs.

Dave acknowledged what he had to do (rule one), accepted his part in it, and tackled it head-on. It wasn't something he had done before, so he did not hesitate to jump to stage three, and ask for help. With the aid of his HR team he came up with a plan he was happy with (rule two), because not only did he do what needed to be done, but he also included counselling for the 50 members of staff who were being fired, and provided advice and resources to help look for a job, which even included time off to attend interviews (rule four). His biggest worry, how to choose the individuals, was taken out of his hands because his company operated a strict first-in last-out policy (rule five).

He didn't think this was particularly fair or even made business sense, but he accepted that this was something he couldn't change. He advocated for more support for the staff and got primarily what he wanted so he changed what he could.

He knew how hard it was going to be for his team, but he also acknowledged how hard it was going to be for him, so he made sure that he removed any other distractions from his routine, tried his best to get as much sleep as he could, which wasn't easy, carried on with his exercise routine, and tried to eat as healthily as he could (rule six).

Finally, rule seven. David was almost reluctant to envisage anything good that could come out of this situation. But there was. Firstly, David did the job with such aplomb and preparation that, everybody, *particularly those most affected by it,* knew exactly where they stood and what was going on, in what time-frame.

Sure, there were a number of unhappy people, of course there were. But at least 20 of those fired got jobs almost immediately with a rival firm, with better pay. Secondly, the people who didn't lose their jobs but were still worried, were made to feel secure and safe in the knowledge that the new structure was a long-term proposal. David told them so and they trusted him.

Thirdly, and David wasn't comfortable with this, he impressed the company he worked for so much that he is now flavor of the month. He received a great appraisal and a pay rise. He did this through proper selfishness. It was a consequence of him thinking the job through, planning and preparing, and looking after himself, as well as the people around him. The more you prepare for challenges ahead of you, the greater your chance of dealing with them well.

Sleep. Eat. Move.

Whether you suffer from negative self-talk or not, looking after your body, treating it with the respect it deserves, also involves looking after your brain and nervous system from whence all your thoughts and feelings spring. As already detailed, all of those thoughts spring from memory banks within your brain and through a series of exquisitely complex electrical impulses. What the brain does, as astoundingly complex as it is, is still a bodily function

A healthy body, therefore, means a healthy mind. And a healthy mind makes you more capable of dealing with challenges, of handling your negative self-talk, and assisting you in changing your subconscious programming.

There are three cornerstones of a healthy body. Firstly, getting enough sleep. Secondly eating the right things, thirdly, getting exercise. Sleep. Eat. Move.

There are volumes of books on sleeping well, eating right and exercising. Feel free to track them down. Here are some valuable pointers to make sure you're on the right track.

Eating well.

Your diet should ideally include lots of healthy

fats and protein, healthy green vegetables, fish, meat, and plenty of liquids. The two major things to avoid are unhealthy hydrogenated fat, the types of fat used by most fast food outlets (because it's cheaper).

The other thing you should avoid, or at least minimize at all costs, is sugar. Sugar in particular is one to avoid because it raises the body's blood glucose levels, the amount of sugar in the bloodstream. The sugar, converted to glucose, is used for energy across the body, but an excessive blood sugar level also inhibits the burning of fat and therefore could lead to weight gain.

Why is this important? Firstly, weight gain, in particular obesity, is associated with a number of chronic conditions including heart disease, strokes and diabetes. Secondly, sugar, through its elevation of blood glucose levels, has a long-term detrimental effect on the brain.

Let's put it this way, diabetes type II is a condition where blood sugar is almost permanently raised, and this has a dangerous effect on all nerve endings, and can lead to amputations, blindness, and impaired brain function. Nowadays Alzheimer's, a debilitating and insidious form of dementia, has recently been given the nickname "diabetes type 3", because of the role high blood glucose levels play.

So, if you want your brain to be sharp and you want your brain to stay fit and healthy, avoid sugar. Government guidelines for sugar are quite low but worth aspiring to. For women it's 20g or 5 teaspoons and for men it's 28g or 7 teaspoons.

Move.

A sedentary lifestyle is another killer. For a healthy body and mind it is essential that you get a range of exercises over a weekly period, including mainly aerobic i.e. ones that exercise the heart, and also some strength exercises.

Lack of exercise has also been linked with heart disease, stroke, and dementia. You should try and exercise for half an hour a day. In case you blanch at that, don't worry. There are lots of things classed as exercise. A good bout of gardening, a nice brisk walk. And of course, sports and running etc. are the activities more traditionally associated with exercise. You don't have to do it all in one go. My friend David from the call center has a brisk walk three times a day for 10 minutes, and at the weekends a longer continuous walk of about an hour or so.

Sleep.

I've saved this till last because it sometimes

87

appears to be the hardest one to control. Many people just report lying down in bed with their minds racing. If this happens, it's a lovely time for your inner critic to keep you company as you lie there, wide awake.

Sleep deprivation is an insidious killer. Unsurprisingly, it's also linked to an increased risk of strokes, heart disease and dementia. Not only that, but a lack of sleep affects you the next day. It affects your cognitive abilities, makes you grumpy, shorter tempered, and if you are prone to bouts of negative self-talk or depression, a lack of sleep is fuel to the fire.

There are things you can do to help yourself get as much sleep as you need, which varies from between six hours a night and 9 1/2, but most people need somewhere between 7 1/2 and eight hours a night. Here's what you can do to help yourself.

- Increase the amount of bright light you experience during the day

- Stop using smart devices an hour before bedtime, thus reducing your exposure to blue light, which impairs sleep

- Stop drinking caffeine late in the day. General guidelines suggest avoiding drinking it about five hours before you go to bed

- A nap is a great thing but not for too long; try and keep it to 20 minutes or less, otherwise it will impact on your night's sleep.

- Try and wake up and go to bed at the same time every day.

- Don't drink alcohol at night, even a small amount. It plays havoc with the amount and quality of your sleep.

- Keep the temperature in your bedroom moderately low. A precursor to falling asleep is a lowering of your body temperature, and if the room is too hot your body cannot get colder

- Keep your room as dark as possible. Invest in a good pair of black out curtains

- Indulge in relaxing activities in the evening such as listening to soft music, reading a book, taking a bath, or meditating. Work out which one is the best for you.

- Make sure your bed is comfortable. This includes the mattress and the pillows.

- Exercise in the day (definitely not before bed). This really helps with your sleep.

- Reduce liquid intake just before bed. I'm not suggesting you become dehydrated, but drinking large amounts of liquid can make you want to go to the toilet in the night, and this can affect your quality of sleep.

- Take a melatonin supplement. Melatonin is a vital cog in falling asleep.

How to Substitute Your Negative Thoughts For Positive Ones.

I have touched briefly on positive self-talk and affirmations, and we are going to talk about those a lot later in the book. Some of you may have already experienced using them. As an example, you may look in your mirror and say to yourself, "I'm so fat and unhealthy." A positive affirmation might be to say to yourself instead, "I am fit and healthy, and I have a lovely body."

But the problem is the conflict between how you feel about yourself (to be more precise how your subconscious is making you feel about yourself) and the words within a positive confirmation. If you look in the mirror and feel fat but then say the words, "I don't feel fat and I am fit", there is a mental sparring match going on between how you feel and the words you say. The words feel almost inauthentic, and it therefore can be a difficult habit to keep repeating them.

Not only that, but your brain will do the easiest thing it can, and your thoughts will drift back to your old negative ways. It's worthwhile repeating once more; these subconscious programs, have been around forever. Ok, maybe not forever, but that's how it can feel. The brain will always go for the easiest option and return to those familiar feelings and thoughts.

Positive self-talk operates within the surface level of your consciousness while the limiting beliefs you are trying to change live in the subconscious. That's why saying something positive that is not actually part of your life script or subconscious programming starts such an inner turmoil.

They can work, because by repeating positive self-talk over a period of time you are throwing in revised programs to your subconscious. Some people report that they work well, but for others, they report that it's just a temporary relief before the old thinking patterns wait for the chink in your armor, and swarm over your conscious thinking. The new positive affirmations just can't hold them back because they haven't established themselves enough in your subconscious.

Furthermore, for people who suffer from anxiety and depression the long-term impact of this conflict can worsen it. But all is not lost.

Start with acknowledging that accepting those thoughts that don't serve any useful purpose beyond keeping you in stasis i.e. where you are. As already mentioned, questioning your inner critic is really powerful, and helps you reframe your thinking in a more positive way. Let's look at this technique in more detail. Here is an inner dialogue related to me by one of my colleagues, with only a small amount of poetic license at the end, added by me!

A Hypothetical Inner Monologue.

Inner Critic(IC): I'm so fat and out of shape.

Questions(Q): Are you? Haven't you lost 6 pounds in the last six months?

IC: Well yes that's true.

Q: So, you're heading in the right direction, aren't you?

IC: Yes, but I'm still big.

Q: But are you heading in the right direction?

IC: Yes, definitely, but it could take a year at this rate.

Q: A year, is that all? How much weight could you lose in the next three months if you carry on doing what you're doing?

IC: 20 pounds.

Q: How's that going to make you feel?

IC: No answer, he's skulked off. For now.

See how powerful it can be? The Process Goes Like this:

Step One. Identify negative thoughts.

Step Two. Ask questions.

Step Three. Reframe that negative thought based on your questions.

Step Four: Say in your head and out loud as many times as you can your positively reframed thought.

Chapter 4: How to Build Self-Confidence

Self-confidence is inevitably severely impacted by those people who have been programed to think negatively of themselves. How can you be self-confident if your inner voice is chipping away at you, telling you that you're too fat, too clumsy, not clever enough, not attractive enough, and all those other debilitating put-downs getting to you?

Self-confidence is of course also related to self-esteem. In fact, the dictionary definition of self-esteem describes it as, "A belief and confidence in your own ability and value" (dictionary.com). Almost certainly if your negative self-talk tells you that you are unlovable, unworthy, or uninteresting then your self-esteem is going to be low, and your confidence is going to be low.

In this chapter I want to talk about confidence itself. Inevitably self-esteem and confidence are closely linked but they are separate things. For example, you may not feel confident enough to go on stage in front of 100 strangers and try and make them laugh, i.e. have a go at stand-up comedy. But that doesn't say anything about your self-esteem.

In fact, lots of comics go on record as saying one of the reasons they go on stage is because they suffer from low self-esteem. Yet all the best comics appear astonishingly confident on stage. In fact, confidence is one of the most important aspects of stand-up comedy.

There is an important point here to be made, continuing the analogy with stand-up comics and stand-up comedy. They appear incredibly confident on stage and therefore appear to have high self-esteem. Yet this is not the case. So how do they do it? I know a stand-up comic, Denny (that's not his real name), who told me that he uses the old cliché "fake it till you make it".

In terms of stand-up comedy, what this means is, despite being racked with self-doubt, you go on stage pretending to be ultra-confident. You do this so many times that in the end you actually do become confident, at least when on stage. But stand-up comics also report that when their confidence skyrockets on stage, it does have an impact on their self-esteem, which improves because they become good at what they're doing.

The Importance of Self-Confidence

Self-confidence isn't just useful for stand-up comics. It will help you in every situation that you can conceivably imagine.

It will help you achieve your goals. Self-confidence is, after all, a comfortable belief in one's own powers and abilities. Confidence itself is defined as the state of being certain about yourself, your abilities, and your status in given situations. This is critical because you need to have a degree of certainty about what you can achieve, because if you don't, and you have in fact uncertainty, how are you going to convince anyone to be certain about you?

Because whatever you do, you will inevitably need to interact with other people, and if you are not certain about yourself you can hardly expect the people around you to be certain about you.

It's important, however, to move away from binary thinking. It's not a case that you are either completely self-confident or completely lacking in self-confidence. Neither is it the case that people are either 100% certain of you or 100% uncertain. Self-confidence is an acquired skill, one which, given time and practice, you will get better at.

For example, one of the shyest people I know is also one of the best plumbers I know. Jill is terrible at interviews and uncomfortable around new people. When applying for a job which would guarantee her lots of work, I suggested she get a testimonial from one of her happy customers, perhaps even write down exactly what she did. She went one better. She took photos on her phone of her next job, and at the interview talked through her last job, accompanying it with step-by-step images.

She reported feeling happy for the first time at an interview. And yes, she got the job. If she was grading her self-confidence at interviews and dealing with new people, she would have scored herself a two or three, but at the nitty-gritty (the plumbing itself) a nine, or even a ten. She successfully transferred some of her self-confidence from one aspect of her life to another. And she continues to work on her people skills, getting more and more confident.

Self-confidence is nuanced, but more of it will definitely help you meet your goals, as you won't be plagued by self-doubt, and you will deal successfully with the people around you.

Self-confidence attracts people too. On the subject of people, when you feel confident, you draw people towards you. People love self-confident people. I'm not just talking about sexual attraction here, though that is critically important. I'm talking about when applying for jobs, waiting for a bus, in your job, or being absolutely anywhere there are other people. Self-confidence will bring people to you.

Self-confidence helps you make the right decisions. When you are self-confident, you choose yourself. Most people who lack self-confidence love to please people. They don't choose themselves, and because of this they make a lot of wrong decisions, or at least decisions that are not as beneficial to them as they could be.

The more confident you are, the more you will feel you have made the right decisions. This works in two ways. Firstly, if you are confident in what you are doing, you're just naturally more likely to make decisions that are in line with your confidence. Being confident means knowing as much as possible what you want.

Also, being self-confident means accepting that sometimes your decisions might actually not be the right ones. Perish the thought, you may have made a mistake. A person lacking in self-confidence and possessing low self-esteem will berate themselves for making a mistake. They'll catastrophize, exaggerate and conduct all the self-talk rituals that I've already discussed in this book.

A person with more self-confidence might be upset, and that's not necessarily a bad thing, but will use his or her upset to learn, and accept that as human beings we all make mistakes. If a self-confident person falls off a bike, they get right up, brush themselves off and get back on.

Self-confidence increases productivity. Again, this works in two ways. A self-confident person is better at making decisions and therefore will be potentially mainly work on things that are helping them to achieve what they want to achieve.

They will be using the time wisely and not even be thinking about other unnecessary activities. A person with less self-confidence, will be uncertain about what they need to do, and therefore won't work as quickly as they might usually do, at least not to start with.

Speaking from personal experience, if you're working on something and you become comfortable with it and you realize it's the right thing to do, while it might take five minutes, an hour, maybe even a couple of days, once you realize you've made the right decision you will become as productive as a fully self-confident person.

But also, a person lacking in self-confidence will be more prone to procrastination and destructive techniques. Social media, TV etc. The problem with getting sucked into a procrastination blackhole is it becomes more and more difficult to stop.

So far all I've really talked about is productivity and achieving goals, but nothing about feelings. Time to change that.

Self-confidence shuts your inner critic down. It's almost impossible to be a self-confident negative self-talker. Self-confidence and negative self-talk are oxymoronic concepts. Self-confidence will quiet down your inner critic, who will sit sulkily at the back of your mind, waiting for a chance to pop up. The more self-confident you are, the less chance it has. Self-confidence reduces negative self-talk, but flip that coin. Positive self-talk helps increase self-confidence.

Self-confidence gives you greater motivation. First of all, the more self-confident you are the more you will get done anyway, because you're not constantly troubled by your self-doubting inner critic. And in a way it's self-fulfilling. The more you get done, the more motivated you become. You'll find yourself doing things that may have worried you previously. Self-doubt will still arise, but it won't be as powerful as it previously was for you.

Self-confidence helps you get back on the bike. A self-confident person will have a much more dispassionate view of when they do something that doesn't quite go their way. I've already mentioned this but it's worth repeating, that a self-confident person puts themselves in a position to truly learn that when things go wrong. When we make mistakes, these are the biggest opportunity to learn something new and worthwhile. Failure therefore leads to growth. The more self-confident you become, the more you even welcome the opportunity of making mistakes. You will rid yourself of the it-has-to-be-perfect syndrome.

In a way the techniques I'm going to discuss are not just designed to help your confidence. Some of them overlap with the tips provided to help improve your mindset.

The more you repeat exercises, the greater the benefit. The tips coming up are designed both to make you feel more confident, but also to make you appear more confident, whatever you feel like. At their heart, these tips also help you jettison some of your falsely held negative beliefs. In a way, you are using a combination of faking it and feeling it. If successful, the overall result will be not just you appearing to be more confident, but genuinely feeling more confident, and thus improving your self-esteem and diminishing your negative self-talk.

Self-Confidence Boosting Tips

- **Use visualization techniques.** Visualizing what you want to be and what you want to achieve is a fascinating process. Visualizing a more confident you can be a fantastic boost, because that visualization triggers the part of the brain that would be active if you were confident anyway. The brain already believes it, and therefore makes you feel better. Visualize yourself socializing at a party and making friends. Visualize yourself presenting to your boss as if you are the king of presentation skills.

- **Reframe your negative thoughts.** We've already touched upon this, but write down those negative thoughts. Don't dismiss them, but reframe them. Come up with a more positive way of viewing them and say those words out loud.

- **Question your inner self.** You are your worst critic but asking questions will not only help you reframe your self-doubt, as already mentioned, but it will also help your self-confidence as you realize that some of your deeply held self-beliefs are simply nonsense.

- Give yourself regular pats on the back if you achieve something well done. This is a way of reinforcing a positive view of yourself.

- **Go on a rejection safari.** This might sound a bit weird, but if you try and make one request every day, the answer to which will almost certainly be no, by the end of the process you should become somewhat desensitized to rejection. What a wonderful quality to have if you are in the dating game, looking for a job, going for a promotion, or being a stand-up comic!

- **Set small, realistic goals.** There's nothing worse for your self-confidence than not achieving your goal. But perhaps you're setting yourself up for failure by setting yourself unrealistic goals. Below, a story.

One of the biggest problems many people have is being realistic in terms of time. Jennifer lived in a house of astonishing clutter. She was a borderline hoarder and knew that it was causing her real problems in every aspect of her life. So, she decided to do something about it.

She binged on Marie Condo and set herself an ambitious plan to declutter and organize herself once and for all. She talked through the plan with me. It was a great plan, one which would have made the house tidy and more importantly would've kept the house tidy.

But here was the problem. She set herself a timescale of a long weekend. She took a Friday and Monday off work, and decided that by the end of Monday she was going to have that house tidy and organized. Problem is, it took a few years for the house to get so untidy, and there was no realistic way she would have completed those tasks within four days, even full-time.

She was depressed and annoyed with herself because she didn't get everything done. But when we talked it through, she realized that what she should've given herself was a month, even two months. Actually, she did an astonishing amount in the four days. She'd made a massive head start. So, thinking about this, she reset her targets to 2 months and achieved everything two weeks ahead of schedule. Her initial target was unrealistic, that was the only problem.

- **Help other people.** Helping other people is a wonderful self-confidence boost. Apart from preventing you from focusing on yourself and your own negative self-talk, actively volunteering to help another individual or a cluster of individuals, whether it be assisting one of your friend's children who is struggling with a piece of homework or volunteering at a soup kitchen for homeless people, it just makes you feel good about yourself and those feelings last for a while.

- **Be properly selfish**. Look after yourself, sleep well, eat well, and move well. Looking after yourself is both a selfish and selfless act, because it makes you better equipped to deal with the challenges that come ahead, and makes you feel much more confident.

- **Practice saying no.** You need to set boundaries here. If your boss asked you to do something that is part of your job then of course don't say no. But if your boss or anybody else at work continually ask you to do things that are not part of your job, because they know you're afraid to say no, then challenge them: say no. You'll be amazed. Suddenly people start respecting you and your boundaries. If the people around you show respect, you begin to respect yourself more

- **Tell yourself every day that you are equal to the people around you.** And you are. Your boss is your boss. That doesn't make him better than you, that makes him in charge of a cluster of people, of which you are one. You are your bosses equal, your colleague's equal, you are your equal to everybody around you. If there's one thing you should tell yourself every day, it's this: Nobody is better than you and you are better than nobody else. On this level playing field the seeds of confidence grow.

- **Fake it until you make it.** I've already talked about that, it's incredibly powerful.

- **Do things to help you relax.** Go out with a friend meditate, read your favorite book, or watch your favorite movie. Doing things that you love helps you relax and will contribute to the overall feeling of well-being.

- **Create and maintain personal boundaries.** This is not just about learning to say no, (an important part of setting boundaries). It's about looking after yourself. The more you look after yourself, the better you feel, the better you feel, the more confident you will remain. In particular you need to create a marked boundary between your work and personal life. I know for many of us this can be difficult, and

I'm not suggesting that you scale down your levels of hard work, if you like to work hard.

Setting boundaries is a difficult task sometimes, but it is critical to maintaining your self-confidence in all areas of life. If you don't disconnect from work, it can lead to conflict and negative feelings.

- **Be true to yourself**. Not automatically going along with what everyone is doing is a repeated message in this book. It does nothing for your confidence and it makes you feel inauthentic. Don't be afraid to speak your mind and stand up for what you think, but don't be afraid to think that other people's ideas are great as well and that you're happy to go along with them. If you're following the crowd, and you will in certain circumstances, it will be for the right reasons (because you agree with what the crowd is doing) not just because it pleases other people.

As an independent author with a small marketing budget, reviews are my livelihood on this platform.

If you are enjoying this book I would appreciate it if you left me your honest feedback.

I love hearing from my readers and I personally read every single review.

Sincerely Yours, Max J. Harrison

Chapter 5: The Importance of Motivation

A simple dictionary definition of motivation is, "A reason or reasons for acting in a particular way." You hear the cliché amongst actors asking about their characters, "But what's my motivation?"

I have motivations for writing this book, you have motivations for reading it. If an individual procrastinates an awful lot he or she has motivations for acting that way. Likewise, negative self-talk is fueled by motivations, most of which reside in the subconscious and we struggle to understand.

Some common reasons to be motivated to do something include:

- Your bladder is full; your motivation is to go to the toilet.

- Your tummy is empty and rumbling, and you are motivated to eat.

- You have an instruction to do something at work. You are motivated by being told what to do by your boss.

- You have bills to pay and therefore you are motivated to do what you're told because you want to keep your job, because the money you get paid pays your bills.

There are thousands of these examples, but I hope you understand that motivation is about why we do what we do. It's not a binary feeling, i.e. you are either completely motivated, or completely unmotivated. You will know this if you have a teenage son who has a chore to do but is more motivated to get on his Xbox. There are some jobs and things that you are more motivated to do and some that you are less motivated to do.

What I want to concentrate on is what I call being highly motivated. Being told what to do by your boss or being paid for something are not the only things that motivate people.

Other than money and being told what to do, people generally use the following words to describe what motivates them.

- A job well done.

- Being part of a team.

- Completing a task

- Meeting deadlines.

- Having nice things.

- Getting recognition and being appreciated.

- A sense of safety and security.

- Competing against other people.

- A feeling of control.

- Prestige and fame.

- Helping others.

- Avoiding embarrassment.

- The desire to change things.

- Learning new things.

- Making sure the people closest to me are looked after.

So, you can see it's more than just about money. For many people it's about helping others, being recognized, or achieving something that makes a difference to other people's lives. It's important you find out what motivates you. What do you want to achieve in life? Knowing this could be the difference between being "normally" motivated, as we all are, and being highly motivated.

The Difference Between Being Motivated and Being Highly Motivated.

There are two types of motivation. There's external motivation, for example, the need to get in to work at a given time because your boss tells you that's when you have to start. External motivation is the amount of salary you get paid. External motivation is any sense of reward, achievement, or satisfaction that derives from outside the individual and his or her psyche.

On the other hand, self-motivation comes from within. A self-motivated individual may have a desire to do something for his own benefit, to change something, to acquire or accomplish something driven by his own feelings and aspirations. Once again this is not a binary debate. There's nothing wrong with external motivation, and it doesn't automatically follow that self-motivation is the be-all and end-all, not if your "self" is motivated to commit crimes or other anti-social acts.

You may have been externally motivated to get that nice job which pays well and means you can put food on the table. But you have pride in your abilities and it's your pride that stems from a sense of self-motivation. This means that the job you were externally rewarded to get is done well by you because you are self-motivated to feel pride in a job well done. Both types of motivation work hand-in-hand.

Other than the anti-social criminality displayed by an extremely small minority of self-motivated people, to achieve success, to be more fruitful in what you do, and to achieve your goals, self-motivation is critical. An internal drive to do what you want to do is paramount.

Then along comes our inner critic again. Self-motivation will always be sabotaged by that old chestnut, negative self-talk. So, whilst you're working on yourself and becoming more confident, hopefully your motivation will improve, but there are specific things you can do to stoke up your own levels of motivation.

In summary, external motivation is useful for doing something that you have to do. Self-motivation is invaluable because you end up doing the things that you want to do.

So, let's look at ways to improve your motivation and boost your confidence at the same time, because they go hand-in-hand.

How being self-motivated helps you have a more positive outlook on life.

Self-motivated people tend to share a few common qualities. First of all, a self-motivated person works harder, gets more done, and doesn't allow distractions to get in the way. In fact, it's not about allowing distractions to get in the way. It's simply a case of not feeling those external distractions in the first place, because you are so self-motivated. When external distractions do come up, a self-motivated person finds it easier to put them back in their box.

Negative self-talk is one of the biggest distractions for those people who aren't self-motivated. A self-motivated person will acknowledge the negative thoughts, but keep pressing on with his or her goal. The negative self-talk becomes less and less powerful.

If you also align self-motivation with the concept of replacing your negative self-talk with positive self-talk, then not only will negative self-talk occur less, but as you automatically replace it with positive self-talk. Its impact on you lessens also. It gets to the point where your subconscious is almost doing the subjugation of the negative self-talk for you. A perfect way to be.

If you're self-motivated, you get more done, not

117

just because you are less prone to distractions, but also because your ability to sharply focus on the task at hand has improved immeasurably. The more you get done, the more you prove to yourself you can get things done.

The more evidence you have of your own capabilities, the easier it is to address negative self-talk and a negative outlook with specific examples of what you can achieve.

Only the most diehard subconscious programming could tell you that you're a failure when the evidence suggests you are highly motivated and hard-working. Still, those programs are clingy, like barnacles on a ship.

It's beautiful really. By working on your negative self-talk, self-motivation, and self-confidence, they all feed into each other, dislodging even the clingiest barnacle.

It is a truism that people with a negative outlook are generally not confident or highly motivated, and that people with a genuinely positive outlook are.

How to work out what motivates you

To understand what will really motivate you need to go deep into what your core values are. A person's core values are their fundamental beliefs and guiding principles. They should influence behavior and help people understand the difference between not just right and wrong but what's right or wrong for them.

It's all about finding out what's the most important things to you. If you find out what's most important to you, then you can find out what motivates you.

Here's how to find this out:

Start by identifying the most important people in your life. It's always great to start with people. Relationships are often the most important thing in the world. But sometimes it's easy to take the people closest to you for granted.

By listing the most important people in your life, you make a conscious effort to recognize and value these meaningful relationships. Since man is a gregarious creature by nature, turning to those closest to you is a practical, effective way to make the most out of life.

Think about the things you enjoy doing the most. Could be anything really. Could be going to wrestling matches, flower arranging, walks in the park, spending time with loved ones, or hiking. By taking the time to articulate what it is you like doing the most, two things will happen.

First, it gives you real insight into the things that motivate you, and secondly it will ensure that future plans will make room for your favorite activities and pastimes.

Think about your qualities, skills, or talents. For people with low self-confidence and negative self-talk this can be quite difficult. The best way to do this is to get yourself an audio recorder (I love this technique. It's the second time it's appeared in this book. That's because it's so effective). Record yourself for just two minutes. In that time say either what you're good at, or recount something you've done well. You cannot be negative, and you're not allowed to quantify anything.

Colin, an associate, did this very exercise , and came up with the following list, in the order it appears here.

Spelling, writing, basketball, football, running, boxing, short stories, public speaking, writing adverts, dealing with confrontation, telling jokes, office organization, project management, looking after children, making children laugh, listening actively, spotting flaws in plans, quizzes, driving, safe driving, making new friends, math, English, History, metabolism, the history of dieting.

Wow, that's some list. And for Colin, he spotted

several things in there that were very important to him. He noticed common themes, like English and writing. Looking after children was a big thing for him, active listening and learning new things also pushed buttons for him.

What have you done that you're the proudest of? In line with analyzing what you believe you do best, take some time to jot down the successes you've had. It doesn't matter if it's a huge accomplishment or something minor. What does matter is the feeling the result gave you. When you're proud and excited about your accomplishments, you experience joy and satisfaction in life. It's also a good hint that these are important to you.

Find out what your family, friends and colleagues think of you. This might sound a bit daunting, but an honest assessment from the people who know you will provide powerful insight. There are four useful questions to pose.

First question - What does (insert your name) think are his/her best qualities?

Second Question- What do YOU think are his/her best qualities?

Third Question - What does (your name here) think are his/her weaknesses?

Fourth Question - What do YOU think are his/her weaknesses?

This exercise serves two purposes. Most importantly, it gives you some real insight from those people who have the most to do with you. You will be surprised at what people tell you with this exercise.

Secondly, it also gives you a powerful view of the difference between what other people think of you and what you think of yourself. If the difference is significant, particularly if you have a lower opinion of yourself than others do, you know just how busy your inner critic has been, and how important it is to dislodge these erroneous images you have of yourself.

Finally, think of a time when you wanted to achieve something but didn't. This might sound a little counter-intuitive, and it's one of the only times in this entire process where it's ok to dwell on negative feelings:

Perhaps you wanted to finish a book but stopped near the end. Or perhaps you finished it but didn't have the heart to send it out to anybody because you were afraid of failure.

Perhaps you saw a dream job, but were put off by the sheer volume of people you knew would be applying. Worse, a colleague you worked with before got the job and you know you're better qualified than him, and you were told by one of the recruiters how disappointed everybody was that you didn't apply, because, on paper at least, you were by far the strongest candidate.

Perhaps a woman you were attracted to for months asked you for a dance at a night out, and you astonished yourself by saying no, and leaving early in a fit of self-disgust.

In case you're wondering, none of the above scenarios are made up. They're from real people with real issues. The point of these exercises is to establish why. Why were you interested in the job/writing the book/the potential romantic partner in the first place? What was it you thought you could bring to the table, could get from the opportunity? Why did you give up before realizing your dreams? What do you remember thinking?

So, know you have a list of reasons you were interested, a list of qualities you believe qualified you for your particular ambition, and finally a list of reasons that prevented you from following through. Which is the more accurate list? If you have the time to do it all again, exactly what would you do this time?

Invariably, everybody who tries this exercise

works out a more positive way to approach the situation, and most importantly, a way of dealing with their inner critic (shouldn't we just call him your inner asshole?) so that it doesn't prevent them from realizing their life's goals.

The end result of this beautifully cathartic exercise is a steel, a resolve, to seize or craft more opportunities. In the end, there is more self-motivation.

What to Do When you Have Found Your Self-Motivation.

You've worked on what deep down pushes your buttons by making a list of things you're good at, and a list of achievements you're proud of (and even the most self-loathing individual will have something he or she is proud of).

You've even solidified this list by asking those people nearest and dearest to you what they think you're good at. Because what you're good at usually stems from what pushes your buttons.

There are some people who hate what they're good at and do it because it gives them other things. Charlie Brooker is a successful British journalist who has gone on to write a number of TV programs. He is the brainchild behind the Netflix sci-fi series *Black Mirror*. Yet he professes to hate writing with a passion, and likens the process to having a bad poo. So why does he do it? He cites two reasons. Firstly, the money, and secondly, the satisfaction he feels when he sees the end product on screen. Brooker is a great writer, but hates writing.

But for most people they usually like what they are good at. In some cases, perhaps they're good at it because they like it. So, you have a list of things that you like and things that you're good at and now a new list.

Now it's time to write down the answers to the following question; What do you want to achieve? It doesn't have to be a big list and it doesn't have to go into fantastic detail at this stage. You could say something like:

- I want to feel secure.

- I want to earn enough money to be able to live in the swanky part of town.

- I want my children to have more opportunities than I did, or the same opportunities as I did.

- I want to play basketball for my local team.

- I want to teach English to college students.

- I want to be a darn good carpenter and make my own things which I can then sell for a profit.

You get the picture.

Now you've got three lists in front of you. Firstly, your achievements list. Secondly, your skills and abilities list and finally your desires list, the one which boldly states your ambitions.

The big question now is do these lists sync, and how do they chime with each other? For example, you may already be writing, and your ambitions list includes writing a novel. The lists resonate completely with each other.

On the other hand, you may have never played basketball before, but you want to play for your local team. You need to assess the gulf between your aspirations and your current situation and if you still think it's worth going for it go for it, you need to make a plan of what you need to do.

By doing this, you are working on your self-motivation by making a thoughtful plan designed to help you achieve your ambitions. Perfect.

Here's an example of somebody using these

techniques. Elsie wants to be an English teacher at the local college. Currently she is educated to degree level but not in English, so she's come up with a plan designed to get her from A to B, A being where she currently is, and B being a teacher at the local High school.

She worked out that the whole venture would take her four years to qualify. She accepted that there might not be a job at the high school after she'd qualified, and was prepared to wait by working elsewhere until one came up.

None of this fazed her, and she set about writing a detailed plan. Here's what she did next, and here's a tip for doing something practical that will motivate you immediately. As well as making the grand plan her final task was making a three month plan starting from that very day - Day Zero, she called it.

Breaking your plan down into bite-size, manageable chunks, and then planning each three months is one of the most effective ways of both getting on with the jobs at hand, while keeping your eye on the bigger picture.

You'll be amazed at how much you keep yourself motivated because it's come from you, within you, but at the same time your plan is a form of external motivation as well.

Daily motivation - what to do when you start losing it.

What I talked about so far is an encouragement for you to take a helicopter view of your life, to set yourself some substantial, achievable goals that you can regularly review and keep focused on. But let's take a more mindful, day-to-day view of things now.

Let's say you're in the middle of a task that's important to you, and your attention starts to wane. You feel tired, you get distracted by a phone call, or, worse, your inner critic comes knocking on your cognitive front-door because he misses you and you haven't played together for quite a while. This is the worst attention sapper, and the biggest motivation vacuum of all. Here's some tips to avoid this happening in the first place, and, if it does happen, to get you back on track.

- Have a break where you do something mildly physical. Studies have shown that short bursts of even the gentlest of activities are good for your heart. Take a five minute walk and see if you can notice something you haven't spotted before. Do the dishes. Tidy your closet. Anything that requires some physical effort.

Then return to your task, hopefully refreshed and ready to start again.

- Have an attitude of expectancy. Wake up in the morning, look at yourself in the mirror, and say, "I expect something good to happen to me today."

- Grant yourself permission to worry about the things you can control, and allow yourself to let everything else gently go.

- Absorb positive information and keep negative information out. From start to finish, if you know the news is going to bother you in the morning, don't read it, or listen to it. Start your day by reading something uplifting and inspiring or remembering something that's inspiring to you.

- If your attention wanes, check your list, see what you've done, and what you want to get done. Sometimes, this is enough to get you back on track.

- Be with positive people as much as you can. Try and avoid the negative Nancy's of the world, and don't allow yourself to get bogged down in malicious or negative gossip about other people.

- Say your positive affirmations out loud. We'll talk about these in more detail in Chapter Seven.

- One of the reasons your attention wanes is because you're bogged down on a particular gnarly aspect of your task. Perhaps there's something that's incredibly painstaking to complete, or something not quite going as you would expect.

In this instance, close your eyes and take four nice, deep breaths. Once you've done that open your eyes and try to get to the root of your issue. If you establish you've made a mistake, that can be quite a relief. With your newfound positive outlook, you can assess and learn from that mistake, and go about your tasks differently.

The mistake could be in your plan. You estimated the task as taking one day but in reality it's going to take three. Congratulate yourself, you've actually made real progress by establishing this fact. Gently re-adjust your time expectations and move on.

- Keep to your plan and constantly review it.

- Pat yourself on the back to celebrate your accomplishments.

- Visualize and rehearse your future achievements.

- Get yourself into a routine. This is something we'll be talking about in the next chapter.

- Stay away from potential distractions. Turn off the internet on your phone. Better still, turn your phone to airplane mode for periods of time. Because if not, you may find yourself sucked into a social media black-hole, or having a quick go on a game. Only the quick go turns into hours and before you know it, half the days gone and your negative self-talk, your inner critic is having a field day. You haven't achieved what you wanted to achieve, and your motivation goes right out the window. Remove these distractions as much as possible. Take structured breaks to stay refreshed and motivated.

- Make a list of the reasons you want to accomplish the particular goal you want to accomplish.

- Chunk your task into bite-size pieces.

- Be prepared to get the help you need.

Chapter 6: Forging Productive Habits and Creating and Maintaining a Healthy Routine

Sticking to a routine allows us to keep habits that support our ambitions and dreams. In addition, a well-considered routine helps us to get rid of our bad, unhelpful habits.

The words "routine" and "habits" are sometimes used interchangeably, yet they are two distinct things.

A habit is an action, an activity, or even a set of thoughts that we repeat over and over. A good routine is a set of habits completed in a specific sequence. The main difference between habit and routine is that habit is a recurrent action with little or no conscious thought, whereas routine requires a high degree of intention and effort.

But habits also inform routines. It's important to

understand this, because adapting new, healthy habits and constructing a routine that supports these healthy habits as well as everything else in your life may just be one of the most important weapons when dealing with and eradicating vicious bouts of self-destructive negative thinking.

The Benefits of a Positive Routine.

"We are what we repeatedly do. Excellence, then, is not an act, but a habit." -Aristotle.

Keeping to a routine every day of the week can be hard work, but having no routine, having no sense of structure, can be far more draining. It can take a mental, physical, and emotional toll on you without you even realizing it. When you don't have a routine, you are subject to the vicissitudes and variations of other people and external events. You are not in control, and there is nothing more draining than the feeling of not being in control. Worse, without a routine your inner critic potentially has free reign to rain all over your day, and appear when it feels like it.

Let's just establish what a good routine is all about. A routine is an amalgam of positively cultivated habits that are all designed to keep you in tiptop condition. These are dependent on your own lifestyle and also what you want to achieve in life, but should involve healthy doses of sleep, rest, and exercise, at least if you want to stay physically and emotionally healthy.

Your routine might include exercising, meditating, tidying up, planning, spending time with your children, listening to music, financial planning, and many other tasks that suit your lifestyle and aspirations. Remember, having no routine does not necessarily mean you aren't carrying out activities that benefit you, but if you are, they will be done in a haphazard, disorganized manner, and will probably fall by the wayside when you get too busy.

But if it's true that a routine is a structured breakdown of healthy habits, let's examine habits first.

The motivational speaker Brian Tracy has this to say: "Good habits are hard to form but easy to live with. Bad habits are easy to form but hard to live with."

If you've not previously put a lot of thought into how you organize yourself, your bad habits have probably emerged organically. Bad habits are hard to replace, but they are replaceable. The good habits you want to adapt require a little bit more thought.

The good news is, it's quite easy to identify your bad or unproductive habits and this is where you should start.

Identifying Bad Habits

Identify your unhelpful habits. Stick them down on a piece of paper or on your computer. Be honest and specific with yourself.

Isabel's bad habit arose when she started working from home. She would work for two hours without a break and then schedule 20 minutes. (The reality is two hours is way too long to work without a break anyway, but that's beside the point here.)

She would watch TV, catch up with personal emails, and go on social media. Twenty minutes would pass, and she would tell herself that an extra five minutes would do no harm. Five minutes later would become another ten, another twenty, and at some stage she would get sucked into that social media black hole, or stuck into a TV series she liked. Before she knew it, she'd been sitting there for two hours and it was lunchtime.

When Isabel finally completed her list of unproductive habits she needed to be very specific about what happened to her, and that's how specific **you** need to be. Write down exactly how long you spend on your bad habit, the impact on your body, your physically and emotionally. Write down the disadvantages of continuing this (or these) habits.

Most of all, make yourself aware of ALL of your habits. If you like to go for a stroll every day, that's a habit. If you go to bed after drinking four cans of extra strong lager, that's a habit too.

The Science of How Habits Form

Forming habits has four chronological steps to it; First comes the cue, then the craving, followed by the response, then finally, the reward. This quartet forms the backbone of each and every habit, in that order. Let's take a closer look at each step.

First comes the cue. It's the cue that's the trigger for your brain to instigate a type of behavior. It is a morsel of information felt by one of the five senses that indicates a reward could be in sight.

There are cues that indicate the location of primary rewards like food, water, sex, and even sleep. Also, nowadays we are conditioned to learn the cues for secondary rewards. By secondary I mean those that don't necessarily arise out of our biological need for survival (sleep, food and drink for individual survival, sex for survival of the species.). Some of the secondary rewards I'm talking about include money, power, love, status, praise, friendship, feeling good, or just personal satisfaction.

The cue indicates how near you are to a reward, and could be as simple as waking up in the morning. That's the cue for some people to have a cigarette. The cue is waking up, the craving for nicotine comes immediately after.

Other cues include the smell of bacon, or the sound of your favorite TV program's theme tune.

Cravings come immediately after the cue, and it's these strong, almost overwhelming desires that are the force that lies behind every habit. Without these cravings to motivate us, the habit would not form. And if your habit is healthier than smoking in the morning, say brushing your teeth, it's not the physical act of brushing your teeth you crave, it's the feeling of a squeaky clean teeth and fresh mouth you crave. If you love a massive breakfast full of sweet pancakes and doughnuts, it's not the pancakes and doughnuts you crave, it's the feeling you get from putting them in your mouth, or the sensation of them passing from your mouth down to your stomach, or that hazy, full feeling you get once you've consumed it, or the sugar rush that goes straight to your brain, or all of these sensations.

Cravings differ from person to person, in two

ways. The cues could be different, and so could what it makes you crave for.

Nick decided to have his Bachelor party in Vegas, much to the dismay of most of his friends. But, his wedding, his rules. Nick is a friend of mine, and that isn't his real name. Our first night was in a restaurant adjacent to a vast bank of noisy slot machines. I watched Nick, fascinated. The discordant jingle-jangle of the machines was at best slightly irritating to me, at worst, a hideous barrage of competing dins.

But to Nick it was a powerful cue. We agreed to have dinner first and then hit the casinos, but Nick fidgeted during the meal, like a child in a candy store. His eyes were drawn by the noise, he was even salivating, and this was before dinner. To him the noise of the slots was a powerful cue to incredibly powerful cravings; to the rest of us it was just noise. Cues like this one are meaningless until an observer runs them though his mental processor and interprets the cue as a craving.

After the craving comes the third stage, the response. The response is the action behind the habit itself. I stress action, but the "action" could be a physical activity, or it could be a train of thought.

Not all cravings translate into responses. It's all

dependent on how motivated you are to do whatever it is you crave versus the amount of effort required to do it. You may have a craving for chocolate chip ice cream. So, you go to the freezer, grab the tub, and chomp away. But if there is none in the freezer, and the nearest open store is a forty minute round-trip, you may not follow through with your craving, in which case it gradually dissipates.

Finally, the response delivers the payback or reward. The reward is the jackpot of every habit. The cue makes you sit up and take notice of the reward, the craving centers on setting up a strong desire for the reward. The response centers around getting the reward. The rewards make us feel satisfied, until the next time. The rewards also instill in us lessons. The brain learns which actions are worth remembering in the future, which actions lead to the reward.

The feelings of pleasure or frustration provide feedback to the brain, which helps it identify useful actions, and pointless ones. With the reward, the habit cycle is complete.

If a type of behavior is thwarted or not fully realized in any of these stages, it will not turn into a habit. If you avoid the cue, the entire process disappears. If the cue occurs but you minimize the craving (for instance, by doing something else to distract you) enough you may not end up following through.

If the craving is strong but you take steps to make it difficult to take the action desired, you might just stop there. For example, if candy is your "poison", you could remove all traces of it from your vicinity, and park your car a 15 minute walk away so you're less tempted to get in it and go to the store.

If you go through the first three steps (cue, craving, response) but the reward doesn't feel strong enough, you'll have no incentive to repeat the behavior.

In conclusion, the cue incites the craving, which leads to a response, which kicks in the reward. These four steps provide the brain with a memory. Repeated a few times, then bingo, a habit is formed.

I have generally focused on unhelpful or unproductive habits like gambling and eating sugary snacks, but there are good habits that help you stay healthy and focused, and bad habits that don't.

If your habit is to swim for 20 minutes a day, that's a healthy habit. But be careful, if a 20 minute swim turns into a four-hour daily stint, then (unless you are a professional swimmer!) that can become an unhelpful habit, particularly if it distracts you from other tasks you need to be doing in your life.

This section is all about changing bad habits and swapping them out for newer, healthier ones, so let's stay focused on bad habits for now.

I have talked about the four steps of forming a habit, but we can call the first two steps, (the cue and the craving) the dilemma stage, and this is when it dawns on you that something needs to change. Your dilemma may be that you need the drink, the junk food, the online gambling session, or whatever the bad habit is. The last two stages, the response and reward, can be called the resolution stages, because this is where you take the action and achieve the change you want, thus resolving the dilemma.

Our behavior is motivated by the desire to resolve a dilemma, and the purpose of every habit is to resolve these dilemmas.

Let's see what this looks like in the real world with a few examples. The first one is incredibly common.

In the dilemma stage.

Cue- You hear your phone buzzing.

Craving - You want to find out what kind of message it is, who sent it, and what it says.

In the Resolution Stage

Response - You pick up your phone and read the message

Reward - You have satisfied your craving. You associate the buzzing cue with picking up your phone and reading the message. The Pavlovian response is in place.

Here's another one.

Cue - You wake up feeling tired.

Craving - You want to feel alert and ready for the day.

response - You drink a cup of coffee, and perhaps another one in quick succession.

Reward - You have satisfied your craving to feel more awake, and now you associate getting up in the morning with an immediate cup of coffee or two.

This habit-forming process doesn't occur if you do something just once. It forms through a few repeats, and it doesn't take long to be classed as a habit.

But most habits form themselves in your childhood. They affect almost everything we do, from which shoe you put on first, to which part of the mouth you start with when brushing your teeth, how you fix your hair, and what you automatically think of when you look at a leaf, or any specific object.

Many of our habits are born when we are young. Happily, we are capable of forming new habits as we get older.

Let's go back to our subconscious, for a moment. Let's consider those life-scripts. If you have been forming habits since you were young, and your actions are dictated by your subconscious, much of your negative responses to events, and much of your harmful self-talk is a habit. Your inner critic is, quite simply, habitual behavior made large.

How to Create Good Habits

We can use our knowledge of these four steps to instill good habits and rid ourselves of old ones. I assume at this stage you have identified what new, healthier habits you wish to acquire, and spent some time identifying unhelpful habits.

So, to create a good habit follow these steps. Let's say you want to introduce 20 minutes of exercise into your morning routine, immediately after your first hot drink. The hot drink is important here, because you need to make the cue obvious and consistent. Let's say the cue is the hot drink, and in particular, the moment you drain the last drop from your cup.

Next stage, the craving. Your exercise is a 20-minute brisk walk. You like walking, and you've studied the benefits of a twenty minute walk each day. After your walk know you will feel more alert and raring to go for the rest of the day. There's your craving right there. That get-up-and-go state of readiness to take on the world. The craving has to be attractive, and that certainly is.

Then you've got the response - the doing part. All you have to do is slip on your walking shoes and away you go. This is critical: whatever the response, it has to be easy for you to do. If it's too much effort, it disincentives you.

Finally, the reward. Your reward, in this instance, is that feeling of alertness you love, and that's important, because the reward has to be, well, rewarding! And when trying to instill new habits, feel free to add rewards as part of the process.

Perhaps you hate tidying but hate untidiness even more. You could instill a reward of a healthy food treat, a refreshing beverage, or 30 minutes of your favorite tv program. Just about anything that is going to make it feel satisfying to you, and something that you can associate with the action of tidying.

So, to summarize the formation of a new habit:

- Create a cue (unlike how your bad habits developed over time, where the cue emerged naturally).

- Work out what you crave. Again, this could be something naturally occurring like the rush of endorphins after exercising, or you could link something else you like, as long as it's healthy. When forming new habits really dwell on how it feels to get that reward. Actively think about it until it becomes a natural craving.

- Respond. It has to be something easy and accessible for you to do.

- Enjoy the reward.

There you have it. Sounds really simple, doesn't it? But that's not all that makes a habit. A new habit is formed through repeating it over and over. For it to really embed itself and become a new habit to replace an old one, you need to repeat it every day for a couple of months at least.

In my personal experience a new habit is only truly embedded after six months. What I mean by truly embedded is that, no matter what stresses you experience during the day, you will still, almost automatically, repeat your new habit.

At the start of the process a "bad" day, whatever that looks like to you, will tempt you to go back to your old ways, but don't be downhearted. Keep at it. After two months you'll be used to your new behavior, and after six months you won't even think about it. You'll just do it!

Learning a new habit is like learning to drive. First you have your lessons and your conscious about what you're doing. Then you pass a test, but you're still hesitant, still conscious about the process. After a few month's practice you get so used to it you stop being conscious of each step in driving. How to do it has now become buried in your subconscious.

How Your Habits Fit into A Routine.

From Tesla to Hawking, Edison to Einstein, most individuals perceived as high achieves had one thing in common, and that is a routine. Every day they did much the same thing at the same time.

I would go so far as to say that instilling positive daily habits within your life is only possible with a regularly planned routine. Following a routine helps you establish priorities, nips procrastination in the bud, makes it easier to track goals, and even makes you healthier. It reduces your reliance on willpower and motivation because habits completed within a well-structured routine start to happen automatically.

Everybody is different, so everybody's routine will be different. However, there are some common features to a routine which will help you in your day and enable you to achieve your goals. Here are some suggestions for your routine. Whether you incorporate them all will be entirely dependent on you.

Start your day with a positive affirmation. Something simple, such as:

- Today is going to be an awesome day.

- I am going to be the best me I can be today.

Something simple and straightforward to start your day, because they put you in the right mindset. Having a positive mindset means that if the day doesn't quite go according to your plan, you are more equipped to cope robustly.

Make your first task a proactive one. Tasks can be divided into two categories - proactive or reactive. Starting your day by checking emails and responding to them is reactive task. The trouble with doing this is that you might encounter an email that you consider needs your immediate attention. You have immediately allowed your day to be controlled by the needs of other people.

A proactive task is one that fits completely in with your main goals. Writing the next five pages of your book, finishing an assignment, studying 20 new words of Spanish vocabulary. If your first task is high on your personal agenda then you are being immediately proactive, and in control. It doesn't mean you won't check your emails, and respond to other people's needs, but you'll do it at a time that suits you, that allows you to still get the important tasks of your day complete.

Read a book. Reading has been scientifically proven to enhance your brain-power. It also reduces the risk of dementia, and helps you relax.

Write. We will be discussing journaling in the next chapter, but writing generally makes you a better communicator and improves your ability to recall important information.

Make a daily to-do list. Keep it small and manageable, and not overwhelming. Try not to have more than six items on your list. Schedule regular breaks. It's overlooked but it can be the difference between achievement and no achievement.

Divide your day into chunks. If you are working on a number of tasks, work on one area for a particular part of the day, and then another for the next part, and so on. This is called chunking.

A different technique for chunking is you could say have Monday for one particular task, let's say writing, Tuesday for editing, Wednesday for chasing business, Thursday for talking to your staff, Friday for planning (obviously these are all examples, so replace the activities with ones that are pertinent to you). It doesn't mean that your day is completely taken by those, you could still get other small tasks done, but your day should generally be dominated by the main theme.

Make sure you keep fit as part of your routine. Also practice deep breathing. Eat well, and drink plenty of water.

Schedule Breaks. It's so easy to forget to do this, but it's vital for your brain and body. The more tired you are, the more of an opportunity your inner critic has of sinking its fangs into your attention.

Get out of your chair as much as you can. Excessive sitting can lead to increased risk of cancer, diabetes, strokes, and heart attacks, so it's in your interest to take five minutes an hour for walking around a bit or doing some stretches.

Learn something new every day. The more you know, the more confident and self-motivated you will be, the easier you will find positive self-talk.

An example of a Pro-active Routine

Mary runs her own business and has three children. Her life is very busy. This is what she does:

5:30 am - Wake up and get out of bed straight away. Repeat positive affirmations for 10 minutes whilst washing and cleaning my teeth. Read inspirational messages.

5:45 am - Read my book. Currently reading *Thinking Fast and Slow* by Daniel Kahneman. Next book on the list is Stephen King's new book. I like to alternate between fiction and non-fiction.

6:15 am - Meditate for 20 minutes

6:35 am - Write my journal.

7 am to 9 am. - Make breakfast for my children, get them ready, play with them, and walk them to school. I love this time I have with them, but I love when they go through the school gates and I have the rest of the day to myself!

9 am to 9:10 am - Review my action list for the day

9:10 to 9:20 am - Positive affirmations

9:20 to 10 am - Complete a challenging task.

10 to 12:30 pm - Work on proactive tasks

12:30 to 1:15 pm - Gym

1:15 to 3:30 pm - Work on the highest priority tasks.

3:30 to 4 pm - Review emails and messages.

4 to 5 pm - Review the day, review my master

plan, and decide on tomorrow's tasks

5 pm - Brisk walk with my family.

5:30 to 5:50 - Meditation

5:50 to 8:30 pm - Spend time with my family

8:30 to 10 pm - Relax, do as I like

10 pm - Brush my teeth, go to bed and sleep.

You'll notice that this routine takes care of business. Mary is developing herself, working hard, ensuring she gets enough sleep, and planning regularly. Her day is full of newly instilled habits, one of them being brushing her teeth regularly because she used to forget and as a result had several fillings. The newly acquired habit of brushing twice a day is embedded into her routine.

This routine works brilliantly for Mary, but unless your life is identical to hers, you'll need to work out your own routine. This may take a few attempts before you get it completely right. That's ok, though. You're learning a new skill here, and making mistakes is part of the learning process. I guarantee you that a well-crafted routine filled with healthy habits will keep that nasty, negative inner critic at bay.

When in Doubt – Always Choose Yourself!

Chapter 7: Journaling

Journaling is an extremely powerful way of challenging and acknowledging your own negative self-talk. It's a way of documenting all of that nonsense your inner critic is saying, with a view to either letting it go or challenging it.

In this chapter, I'm going to talk about the differences between journaling and writing a diary, the role journaling can play in moving from a negative to a positive mindset, whether you should hand write your diary or use some other means, and when to write it. I'm also going to give you examples of two different types of journals: The stream of consciousness journal and a type of diary used by people who want to reframe negative self-talk, the cognitive journal. I'm also going to leave you with a prospective journal plan for you to start the process.

Journals and Diaries

The words journal and diary are frequently used interchangeably across literature. Generally speaking though, they do serve different purposes. A diary is more about the specifics of what happened during the day, or what is going to happen. 10 o'clock had a meeting, 12 o'clock - lunch with the boss, 1 o'clock, saw an accident et cetera. They record what has happened in the past and are a useful guide for tracking what's going to happen in the future.

A journal, however, is much more about how events made you feel, and how you reacted, rather than a record of the event itself. Plus, a journal is rarely, if ever, used to plan something in the future.

A journal encourages you to hone in on your largest feelings. Consequently, not every event will make it into there. A journal is far less planned as well. In fact, the best way to write a journal is to start it with no preconceived notions of what you're going to write. Treat it as a stream of consciousness. If you're sitting in front of blank page, not sure where to start, write exactly what you can see and take it from there. If you see a banana, describe it. As soon as you start writing you'll be surprised in the direction it takes you.

From the point of view of changing your negative outlook on life, and your negative self-talk, a journal can be invaluable. It's a true, real-time record of what and how you're feeling. By writing exactly what's on your mind you get to see the words of your inner critic, right there in black-and-white.

There are people who say that merely by writing down their negative feelings makes them feel better. Journaling like this can help them actively concentrate on thinking more positive thoughts. But there are others who prefer a bit more of an action-based approach to the whole journaling process. Before we talk about Cognitive Journaling there are a few other questions to address.

Handwriting versus typing.

There is a school of thought that says you should only write a journal by hand. There are definitely some advantages to doing this, but there are also disadvantages. There are other ways of writing a journal, including a word processor on your laptop, dictating it using voice typing, writing on a smart application by tapping your fingers on the screen. The key thing is that you should be doing writing a journal, no matter how you write it. There may be some advantages to handwriting it, but writing a journal by any means is better than not writing one at all.

The big advantage in handwriting a journal is that more of your brain is being used. There's a more complex relationship between your hand, the pen or pencil, the paper, and your brain than there is using a standard computer keyboard or touching a screen.

Writing with a pen and paper feels more personal, and of course you don't have to worry about getting hacked. But the problem with writing by hand is that it's just not just not as quick, and it's physically hard, particularly for people with arthritis in their fingers and wrists.

Generally, writing by hand forces you to slow down, and if you're writing a novel or anything that needed consideration this might be to your advantage, but writing a journal where you're writing a stream of consciousness about your feelings means that you want to get the words down as quickly as possible, before use lose them from your stream of consciousness.

It can also be messy. Many people tell me that they started writing a journal by hand but stopped when they realized that they couldn't read their writing a few days later.

It's a beautiful way of doing it, but don't be too bogged down by a particular method; just write a journal.

When and How to Write a Journal

A good time to write a journal is when it suits you. If you're a morning person, do it in the morning. An evening person, the evening. But what's also useful is to have access to your journal all day. If something happens that feels big to you, stirring emotions, and making you upset, that's a perfect time to take ten minutes to write it all down.

What exactly are you going to write in your journal? The biggest thing is not to worry about recounting the exact details of specific events. You only need to do that if those particular events incite emotions and feelings in you.

Let's play with an example. Here's how a diary might look.

Went to see the Rolling Stones with my wife. We took the 8.10 bus to the stadium, which ran late. So, when we got there the support band were on. Somebody called the Tea-timers. Never heard of them. I will look them up tomorrow. The concert was good. They played the song "Angie" and it reminded me of an old girlfriend. The concert finished at 10:40 and we just caught the last bus home.

Here's how a journal might look.

At the Rolling Stones concert, they played the song Angie, and it made me think of my first love, Carol. Thirty years ago, we'd dance around our apartment to that song. God, we were in love. God, I treated her badly. I can still smell her hair. Hearing that song made me feel sad and a bit lost. My wife asked me if I was alright, and that just made me feel guilty because I was moping over a woman I haven't seen for thirty years, when next to me is this beautiful woman. And then I felt worse because I started comparing Carol to my wife.

The difference in emphasis is vast here. The second entrance is full of feelings, and a heavy dose of negative self-talk which the writer can unpick later.

After a while the writer would be able to see a pattern of triggers that make his negative self-talk kick in. That's when he can really start tackling his inner critic head-on.

For many this type of journaling works brilliantly, and goes hand-in-hand with positive affirmations in freeing oneself of all the negative nonsense stored up over the years within your psyche.

But for quite a few people this stream of consciousness writing can have a detrimental effect. Let's say you're writing a journal about how particular situation made you feel. Could be anything like something your partner or boss said to you, or a road-rage incident.

The situation made you feel awful. It made you feel as if you were a total failure and a complete loser. For some people, documenting these words, writing them down and seeing them can merely confirm what they feel about themselves and can easily throw them into a negative cycle of writing, and a negative spiral of bad thoughts. It's possible to write one of these journals and actually feel even worse. I stress, not everybody feels this way, but for those who have tried it, there is an alternative approach out there. It's called cognitive journaling.

Cognitive Journaling

Cognitive journaling belongs to a form of psychotherapy called cognitive behavioral therapy or CBT for short. It's currently all the rage and has been for about 20 years.

One of its appeals for both therapist and client is that it takes a more direct and speedier approach to resolving issues. It's far more direct, then, say, the approach taken by Freudian or Person-Centered psychotherapy.

In order to explain and understand cognitive journaling, it's important to understand some of the basics of CBT principles. One of the great things about the CBT approach is that it really helps when reframing negative self-talk.

The cognitive journaling method is the brainchild of a European doctor, Richard Ragnarsson. Before we get into the journaling itself, let's start by looking at one of the founding techniques of cognitive behavioral therapy.

The ABC model of cognition.

In this instance, ABC stands for **A**ctivating event, **B**eliefs and **C**onsequences. The CBT model of therapy believes that all experiences in life can be divided into these three different areas.

A- The activating event. This is any occurrence or event in your life that sparks off a chain or a series of thoughts feelings and emotions. It could be an internal event, like the realization of something. It can also be an external event and in most cases much of negative thinking comes from something that happened to you externally. Examples of an activating event are, well, absolutely anything like somebody near you eating an apple, children crossing the road, or a crossword with your sister.

B- The belief. This is our beliefs, the conclusions we draw about and around the activating event.

C- The consequences. This is the upshot of your beliefs about the activating event, the feelings and emotions that follow as a result of your beliefs.

In summary, our thoughts are derived from our feelings, opinions and beliefs about something that happened to you and we act on those thoughts. This also explains why some people react in different ways to the same events because they have different feelings and thoughts.

Let's use an example. You walk down the

corridor at work and in the opposite direction is your boss. "Good morning", you say cheerily. Your boss barely acknowledges you, doesn't say a word and doesn't even look at you properly. He looks really unhappy. Boom, that is the activating event - your boss' response to your good morning.

This disturbs you enormously. You start asking yourself - why did he ignore me? Why was he so unfriendly? What have I done? My appraisal is coming up in three day's time. What does this say about that? You feel nervous, anxious, annoyed, angry, and sad all at the same time. This is because you believe your bosses response relates to you, and only you. It occurred as a result of something you have done. These are your beliefs.

The consequences, your negative feelings, lasts for hours, possibly days. You can't concentrate at work because you keep getting upset. It affects your sleep and you are a tornado of worry.

The problem with these consequences is that we never stop to scrutinize the belief part of this process. We never apply any logic to it. We go from activating event, automatic beliefs and awful consequences with lightning speed.

And your thoughts, your conclusions, and the consequences of those conclusions become activating events in themselves because they get you locked into a spiral of negative thoughts, locked into a helplessly downbeat mentality.

That's what cognitive behavioral therapy is all about - examining those negative beliefs and reframing them.

In this example let's go through the process again.

Stage one - Your boss doesn't acknowledge your cheery good morning.

Step two - This triggers a whole pile of negative and worrying beliefs about yourself and your relationship with your boss that get worse and worse.

Step three - The consequences are feeling bad for days on end, worrying, and just feeling awful. You don't want to talk to your friends, or your family when you feel this way.

Now, let's jump back to stage two. Before allowing yourself to be immersed by the consequences, stop and ask yourself some questions. Write them down to help you process. Some of the questions you could ask include:

- Do I really know why my boss acted that way?

- Do I have any idea about how my boss feels about me?

- What is my relationship like with him generally?

- What evidence do I have that what happened means I'm going to get a negative appraisal?

- What evidence do I have that I'm going to lose my job?

- What evidence do I have that my job is safe?

This line of questioning should at least shift your beliefs as you work out that you have no idea why your boss acted that way. You generally have a good relationship with him, you have no idea about your appraisal, though you have a good feeling about it, and you have zero evidence you're going to lose your job. In fact, you just got promoted, remember?

You could, if you still need to, make a list of reasons he acted that way. He was tired, he had an emergency, he was in a bad mood with everybody, he didn't hear you, he had something on his mind, and he was focused on that. It turned out that your boss had just found out that his wife had been in a car accident. Nobody was hurt, but his wife was shaken up and upset, and he was rushing to go and help her out.

So, there was a logical reason why your boss ignored you. But what if there wasn't? Sometimes people act in ways that don't stand up to logical scrutiny. But this doesn't mean you have to go all Chicken Licken on yourself (The sky is falling! The sky is falling!).

What the ABC model does is help you understand that you can influence your thoughts about events in your life by changing your beliefs. And this process underpins the cognitive journal.

How the Cognitive Journal works.

The cognitive journal initially works like a stream of consciousness journal. You can write something down spontaneously. You don't have to worry about grammar, punctuation, or anything like that. Nobody will see the journal, unless you choose to show somebody.

You can really examine an event and how it made you feel. Unlike the stream-of-consciousness journal, once you've written it you stop any downward spiral dead in its tracks by examining the beliefs around the event that triggered your feelings.

Where this really powerful technique comes into its own is your chance to examine in detail your beliefs, expose flawed beliefs about yourself, and reframe those beliefs into more positive and realistic ones. And it's from here your positive self-talk will flow. Doing this silences your inner critic.

Dr. Ragnarsson (Power of Positivity, 2009) claims that other types of journaling prevent us from changing the way we think because it reinforces, rather than challenges our negative self-beliefs. What he suggests is a practice program to get you started, so here goes:

WEEK 1: MAKE JOURNALING A HABIT

Firstly, pick one memorable recent event in your life. It could be a huge event, or it could be a small one, it really doesn't matter. Write it down in as much detail as possible. Try to be non-judgmental and factual when writing it down. You are now going to examine this event through the lens of the ABC model, but you're going to start with the consequences first, followed by the activating event, and finally, a deep examination of the beliefs triggered by the event.

It should look something like this:

C (Consequences) - I felt (write down your

feelings and emotions here). What I did was (write down your actions/behaviors here).

A (Activating Event) - What happened was [insert details of what happened here].

B (Belief) - This made me think [insert your beliefs, opinions and thoughts here].

Get into the habit of writing at least one sentence within this structure at least once every day. In this first week, don't worry about trying to reframe your thoughts and feelings. Just get used to the technique, and get comfortable with documenting events and recording your feelings through the lens of the ABC model.

WEEK 2: Pinpoint Those Beliefs

In week 2, add to your cognitive journaling by devoting some time each day to identifying and analyzing your beliefs. One-by-one pick each belief and write it down. Read it out loud. Study it like you would study a piece of art. Then ask yourself some logical questions about the accuracy of these beliefs, again one-by-one. Also, ask yourself if these beliefs are helping you or hindering you from achieving your goals. And ask if the feeling these beliefs spawn are productive or useful in any way. Also, try and spot any discernible patterns in your beliefs in similar

171

situations.

WEEK 3: Ask Deeper Questions of Your Beliefs

While carrying on the process started in week one and added to in week 2, it's time to seriously challenge those faulty beliefs of yours.

To each belief pose these questions:

- What logic is there in this belief?

- What evidence supports this belief?

- What evidence supports the notion that this belief is false?

- Is this belief any use to me?

If your belief stimulates a positive feeling, you will easily be able to establish its logic, identify supporting evidence, and pinpoint how it serves you. But if the belief is a negative one, it will become startlingly apparent. There will be no logic to it, there will be no evidence, except evidence that demonstrates its falsehood. And the answer to the last question, is this belief any use, will be a resounding no.

Finally, write down how this particular part of the process makes you feel.

WEEK 4: Constructing Helpful and Realistic

Beliefs

After pinpointing, interrogating, and exposing the unhelpfulness and inaccuracy of your faulty beliefs, now is the time to reframe those bad beliefs, and construct new ones that will help you move forward in your life.

See if you can come up with two or three replacements to your bad beliefs about each event.

Ensure that your beliefs are logical, helpful, and easy to demonstrate. You have reframed your negative self-talk!

Now, go back to the work you started in the first week, insert one of your reframed beliefs into the scenario, and kick out the bad one. See how that makes you feel. If you feel good, use this new belief the next time you are in a similar scenario.

Summary

Cognitive journaling can provide tangible advantages to anybody plagued with negative feelings towards themselves. In order to get real benefit from it, you need to start it now, and do it every day. It will encourage you to challenge every faulty view you have of yourself. It can also help you devise some brilliant positive affirmations totally personalized towards you. More on that in the next chapter.

Chapter 8: Positive Affirmations that Work for You

In this chapter we are going to discuss how positive affirmations fit into the raft of activities you can do to help replace your negative thoughts with positive ones.

Positive affirmations are an ideal and easy way to re-train your negative subconscious programming. The theory is that the words, repeated often enough over a period of days, weeks, or even months, will start to embed themselves into your life-scripts, and genuinely change the way you think, and therefore the way you feel about yourself.

There are three types of affirmations you could try.

The first type is generic, off-the-shelf, and available from many websites.

For example, I typed into Google a random search on positive affirmations. There were

174

literally hundreds of sites to choose from. I chose a site called As the Bird Flies (I will provide the full web address in the reference part of this book). They list one hundred affirmations for various situations, including affirmations for mood boosts, ones to help you at work, ones to give your creativity a boost, and many other categories. I've picked three at random. Here they are:

- My smile makes others smile.

- I work hard and know my worth

- I share what I create with pride and grace.

There are hundreds on this website, and hundreds of websites offering the same types of affirmations.

The second type are affirmations that are tailored to you. The affirmations above are all well-and-good, but how relevant are they to you? What you can do is, either, trawl through these websites and identify ones that resonate with you, or you can write your own.

If you've started journaling you will now have identified what your main sources of your negative self-talk are. If you're worried about your weight, you could write some aspirations to negate this worry, such as:

- I am the best physical version of myself I can possibly be.

- Everything about my body is beautiful.

- I am not overweight, I am the perfect weight for who I am.

The third type, we'll come on to a bit later.

The Problem with Affirmations.

The problems with the first type of affirmations, even the ones that resonate with you, is that they potentially set up an emotional conflict. I have spoken in some detail in my chapter on Changing Mindsets, specifically in the section "How to Substitute Your Negative Thoughts for Positive Ones." I describe the conflict between what you say, the positive affirmation, and what you truly believe.

Let's say you look in the mirror and say to yourself,"I'm such a fatty!" and you decide to replace those words with one of the positive affirmations above. You go for "I am not overweight, I am the perfect weight for who I am."

But what if your subconscious programming forces you to condemn your overweight self, by making you truly, consciously believe that you are a "fatty" and this is a problem because other people notice how fat you are. So, there's no point meeting anybody, or going anywhere other than the places you have to, you mother's, and your place of work.

It doesn't matter if these beliefs are true (they clearly aren't). Your genuine belief, fueled by your subconscious, believes it to be true. So, if you come along and boldly state in the mirror, "I am the perfect weight for who I am," your subconscious rebels and sends you contrary messages. For some people repeating lines like this can work, but for many, all it does is set up a conflict between what you genuinely believe, and the words you say repeatedly. In some instances, they can make things worse.

So, now we come to the third type of positive affirmations, ones that are created by you as a result of reframing your negative self-talk.

If you have read the chapter on Mindset, or taken part in the cognitive journaling exercise in the last chapter you will already have written down a stack of re-framed beliefs that would make ideal positive affirmations. But if you haven't, no matter. You can jumpstart the process by reviewing the ABC model of cognitive therapy in chapter seven. Identify some of your negative beliefs, really start to question their logic, and then come up with your own tailor-made, reframed positive affirmations.

For example, let's look at the person with the weight issues above. His beliefs about himself fall into two categories. Firstly, he believes he is overweight. Secondly, he believes that people notice that about him, and will not want anything to do with him. Therefore, he believes the sensible course of action might be to just avoid extra social contact as much as possible.

Let's look at his first belief. This individual might apply some logic to it, and there he finds that his doctor supports his belief, and has warned him about all the health risks associated with obesity. He's presented with a chart that states he is on the foothills of obesity. He is presented with the evidence that he gets out of breath at the mildest amount of physical activity. All of this evidence might confirm his belief. But wait, this very act may encourage him to start an exercising and following a weight-loss program.

Now, let's look at the second set of beliefs. After examination, he realizes that there is almost no evidence to support his contention that a) everybody has noticed his weight gain and b) nobody wants anything to do with him so it's best to stay in. In fact, when he thinks about it, people like his company, and have in the past called him a good listener.

Now, he can create as set of positive affirmations that have both reframed his negative beliefs and feel much more genuine to him. They could be something like this:

- I am a really good listener, and people enjoy my company.

- I have a set of great friends who love spending time with me.

- I have so much to offer to everybody.

- I am working hard to become healthier.

He could write loads, and notice there's even one which acknowledges how he feels about his weight, but pats himself on the back for doing something about it.

Try it yourself. If you've already reframed your negative self-talk, write some affirmations on post-it notes, or cards. If you haven't, go ahead, try one. The affirmations you come up with will resonate with you on a much deeper level.

How to Make Positive Affirmations Stick

If you have been through the reframing exercises and have come up with a cluster of affirmations, then you're off to a great start, because the more you personalize them the greater chance you have of remembering them. Also remember to:

- Make them memorable. Don't make them too long. Make them punchy and to the point.

- Keep it positive, keep it present. Don't have an affirmation which says, "I will stop doing this, or I will no longer do that." Instead dwell on your new positive behavior. Instead of, "I will stop eating doughnuts", say "I love eating healthy soups." Also, don't refer to the past or the future; make the affirmations present tense. "I am working hard today."

- Repeat three times a day. Ten minutes at a time, once in the morning, once in the middle of the day, and once before you go to bed.

- Really feel what you are saying. Visualize it, imagine touching it, feeling it, smelling it, whatever is appropriate.

In summary, regularly repeated affirmations that are geared around your life and designed to counter your negative beliefs, can make a big difference in reprogramming your faulty subconscious thinking

When in Doubt – Always Choose Yourself!

Conclusion

In this book, I have provided you with a huge wealth of information and advice to help you kick your negative outlook, your negative self-talk, your inner critic, whatever you want to call it. We've looked at how to start believing in yourself, and to always choose yourself.

If you've read this book from cover-to-cover, you now know just how destructive negative thinking can be to your emotions, your health, and even your wealth. You also know how neuroplasticity gives us real hope to change your negative thinking. Your understanding of the subconscious, and your programming will have given you real insight into why people think the way they do.

Also, this book gives you all the tools you need to recognize your own negative programming and then swap a negative mindset for a positive one. You'll also understand how important self-confidence and motivation are to a healthy positive outlook on life, and how they all go hand-in-hand.

Finally, you'll now understand how to forge

productive habits, create healthy routines and positively reframe your negative thoughts by swapping them out for positive thoughts using journaling and positive affirmations.

Some final advice

- Don't rush into things. Take some time to consider which of the interventions I have described will work for you. Try some out, before landing on the approach that suits you.

- Don't expect quick fixes or miracles. The habits of negative self-talk you are trying to shed took seed in your childhood and have only grown since then. How old are you. In your twenties? Then they've had a decade for them to take root. In your forties? Three decades. Don't worry, digging up the roots of negative self-talk won't take as long. But it won't happen overnight either. Be patient with the process, and be patient and kind with yourself.

- If there's one part of this entire process I implore you to become familiar with, it's the techniques described in chapters seven and eight, (Journaling and Positive Affirmations) on how to reframe your negative thoughts. The more you practice those techniques, the better, and quicker, you will become at it. Eventually, you'll get so good your inner critic might even lose interest.

If you follow this book and this advice, you'll be amazed at the difference it will make in your life. You'll feel like a better you, you'll achieve more and feel great. Good luck.

Thank-you for purchasing and reading this book. Feel free to leave a favorable review.

When in Doubt – Always Choose Yourself!

As an independent author with a small marketing budget, reviews are my livelihood on this platform.

If you are enjoying this book I would appreciate it if you left me your honest feedback.

I love hearing from my readers and I personally read every single review.

Sincerely Yours, Max J. Harrison

Bibliography

Alexander, R. (2011, Aug 15). 5 Steps to Make Affirmations Work For You. Retrieved from https://www.psychologytoday.com

Bass, M. (2018, November 01). Daily Positive Affirmations List and How to Write Your Own. Retrieved from https://mindtosucceed.com

Berne, E. (1961) Transactional Analysis in Psychotherapy. New York. Grove Press.

Fuchs,E. (2014, Apr 04). Adult Neuroplasticity: More than 40 years of Research. Retrieved from www.hindawi.com

Glei, J. (2012, Oct 02). Hacking Habits: How to make New behaviors Last For Good. Retrieved from www.99uadobe.com

Gotter, A. (2018, June 27). Fixed Mindset and Growth Mindset. Retrieved from www.thepeakperformancecenter.com

Handy, C. (1994).The Empty Raincoat. London. Arrow

Hanson, R. (2019). The Neuroscience of Lasting

Happiness. Retrieved from www.rickhanson.net

Komninnos, A. (2017, August 07). How Emotions Impact Cognitions. Retrieved from https://www.interationdesign.com

Larkin, P. (2001).Collected Poems. New York. Farrar, Strauss and Giroux.

Morin, A. (2017, August 29). What Mentally Strong People Don't Do. Retrieved from https://www.psychologytoday.com

Morin, A. (2018, May 09). The beginner's guide to changing Negative Thoughts. Retrieved from www.psychologytoday.com

Morin, A. (2018, Nov 29). A Simple But Effective Trick to Stop Worrying So Much. Retrieved from www.pyschologogytoday.com

Power of Positivity (2009). Psychology Explains How 'Cognitive Journaling' Can Stop Negative Thinking. Retrieved from https://www.powerofpositivity.com

Smruti, G. (2017, May 16). The Secret to make Affirmations Work For You. Retrieved from https://true-connection.org

Sun, J. (2016, Jan 16).Mindfulness in Context: A Historical Discourse Analysis. Retrieved from www.researchgate.net

Tarle, I. (2016, Nov 08). Why is Journaling no.1Hack Against Overthinking and Low Self-Esteem. Retrieved from https://medium.com

Thompson, F. (2018, August 20). Self-Love. List of 100 Daily Positive Affirmations. Retrieved from https://asthebirdflies.com

Widrich, L. (2014, April 02). What Happens To Our Brains When We Exercise And How It Makes Us Happier. Retrieved from https://fastcompany.com

Wilding, M. (2016, Aug 15). Forget Positive Thinking: This is How To Actually Change Negative Thoughts For Success. Retrieved from https://forbes.com

Winfield, C. (2018, Jun 21). The Ultimate Guide to Becoming Your Best Self. Retrieved from www.open.buffer.com

Wong, K. (2017, May 03). Journaling Showdown: Writing vs. Typing? Retrieved from www.lifehacker.com